THE SHAKSPERIAN STAGE

A Typical Shaksperian Stage—Perspective View

THE
SHAKSPERIAN STAGE

BY

VICTOR E. ALBRIGHT, Ph.D.

AMS PRESS INC.

New York, N.Y. 10003

1965

Reprinted with the permission
of
Columbia University Press

1965

AMS PRESS, INC.
New York, N.Y. 10003

Manufactured in the U.S.A.

TO

THE MEMORY OF MY FATHER AND MOTHER

PREFACE

In the Introduction to *A Typical Shaksperian Stage*, published in January, 1908, it was stated that the text was "a portion of a study of the Shaksperian stage soon to be published." The study is now completed, and the earlier essay forms the third chapter. The outline of the work is the same as previously given, except that what was originally intended for the fourth chapter is here divided into three chapters.

I gratefully acknowledge the assistance which I have received in the course of this investigation. Professor J. W. Cunliffe kindly aided me in securing some material from the British Museum. Professor Edward Dowden and M. J. J. Jusserand gave me several valuable references. To most of the men of the English Department of Columbia University I am indebted: to Professor Brander Matthews for suggesting to me the subject of the Shaksperian stage, for various suggestions and criticisms during the course of the work, and for the inspiration and general stimulus which I have received from his courses in the Drama; to Professor W. W. Lawrence for a careful reading of my manuscript; and especially to Professor Ashley H. Thorndike, who has been my constant adviser throughout this study,—to him

> "Only I have left to say,
> More is thy due than more than all can pay "

V. E. A.

Grantwood, New Jersey
    June 22, 1909.

CONTENTS

LIST OF ILLUSTRATIONS

THE SHAKSPERIAN STAGE

————

INTRODUCTION

THIS study is an investigation of the structure of a typical
stage and of the general method of play-production in the
Elizabethan period. The materials which have been used are
mainly of four kinds: 1. Contemporary statements and
records bearing on the stage. 2. Four drawings which have
usually been considered as presentments of interiors of Shaksperian theaters. 3. Pre-Elizabethan and Restoration stage
conditions. 4. The Elizabethan drama.

The first consists mainly of the contracts for constructing
the Fortune and Hope theaters, and of Henslowe's *Diary*.
The Fortune contract gives us considerable information about
the main building, but unfortunately almost nothing about the
more important features of the stage. We are told that the
stage was forty-three feet wide, extended to the middle of the
yard, was partly covered by a "shadow," was paled "with
goode stronge and sufficyent new oken boardes," and contained
posts which were "square and wrought palaster-wise, with
carved proportions called Satiers, to be placed and sett on the
topp of every of the same postes." We are thankful for thus
much information, but we cannot reconstruct a stage from it;
we must first be able to understand all that is implied in the
sentence, "And the said stadge to be in all other proportions
contryved and fashioned like unto the stadge of the saide
Playhouse called the Globe." The same indefiniteness and
disappointment are met in the Hope contract.

The old drawings would be conclusive evidence of the structure of the stage were it not for the fact that there are serious objections to each one. The Swan picture cannot be accepted in all its details; the so-called Red Bull is perhaps a presentment of a Commonwealth stage; the Messallina and Roxana do not in either case show a complete stage.[1] Under such conditions, these pictures must be used with great caution.

A knowledge of the stage conditions before and after 1576–1648 is of more value than either the drawings or the contemporary statements. Dramatic customs in any age or nation change very slowly: while a new play is being written, an old one is being played; and the new and the old are adapted to the same form of stage. One by one, however, certain features are discarded and others added, and after centuries have gone by a new form of stage and a new method of play-production are found. There were no permanent playhouses before 1576, but there were certain laws of staging which were usually adhered to; and after the Elizabethan period there were permanent theaters and definite principles of staging. Therefore, an evolutionary study of this subject is possible, and must yield valuable results.

But of all the sources of information, the plays are the most important. Contemporary statements may be misinterpreted, the old drawings may not be reliable, even the regular development of the English theater may be questioned, but the great Elizabethan drama has forever stamped upon it a picture of the old outer-inner stage upon which it was played, and the laws under which it was performed. One cannot, indeed, read these facts as one runs, nor obtain the whole truth from a few plays; but by a consistent study of the main body of plays, one may form a definite idea of the principal features of the stage and the general method of play-production.

The Elizabethan plays to which I have given special study and from which I have selected the majority of my illustrations are those of the well-known dramatists of the period,—Lyly,

[1] For a full explanation of these pictures see Chapter III.

Peele, Kyd, Marlowe, Greene, Lodge, Shakspere, Jonson, Chapman, Dekker, Marston, Middleton, Heywood, Beaumont and Fletcher, Massinger, Webster, Ford, Shirley, Davenant. Few quotations, however, have been taken from Shakspere. My reasons are that plenty of proof can be found for the main points at issue outside of his pieces, and, more especially, that I have in hand a special essay on the staging of Shakspere's plays.

In selecting illustrations from the Elizabethan drama, I have asked myself but three questions: 1. Was the play, from which the illustration is taken, written in the period 1576–1642? 2. Was it written for one of the regular public or private theaters? 3. Was it a normal play? Other questions concerning dates of performance and publication, and theaters at which the plays were produced, have not entered, and, as I conceive the matter, should not enter this discussion of principles and typical conditions.

As I do not discuss this matter of dates and different theaters elsewhere, perhaps a few words may be needful here. A continuous reading of the Elizabethan drama shows clearly that all the regular, normal plays of the period were written for the same form of stage. As William Archer says, "The more one reads of the Elizabethan drama with a view to reconstructing its material mechanism, the more is one conscious of a certain 'standardisation' of effects. . . . The tendency of investigation is . . . to encourage the belief that the great majority of dramatists, in constructing their pieces, kept in view a normal or typical stage."[1] Undoubtedly the eleven or twelve theaters differed in minor details; but the main parts—the parts which were vital to the dramatists in their workshops—were the same in all regular theaters for at least the last sixty years of the period.

There were, of course, other stages besides the normal ones in England during the Elizabethan period. There were special stages at the Court and the homes of the noble families for the performance of masques, pastorals, and the like ;and also stages

[1] "Elizabethan Stage ", *Quarterly Review*, April, 1908.

at the universities and elsewhere for the dramas of Seneca, Plautus, and Terence, and English plays modeled on them. As to the performance of court masques, I need only to refer to Mr. W. J. Lawrence's valuable article, *The Mounting of the Stuart Masques*, in *The English Illustrated Magazine* for November, 1903. The stage for the Plautine comedies may claim a word of explanation here. It consists of an open space representing a street, yard, square, etc., before one or more doors which stand for entrances to houses. All the action takes place on this neutral ground. The characters are called out of the houses, ordered to appear at this particular place, or chance to be passing by. For example: in *Miles Gloriosus* the scene represents a street before the houses of Periplecomenus and Pyrgopolinices; in *Menaechmi*, a street before the houses of Menaechmus and Erotium; in *Amphitryon*, a yard before the house of Amphitryon; in *Andria*, a street before the houses of Simo and Glycerium. No stationary properties are used except chairs, benches, and such things as might naturally stand before any house. The structure of this stage is so evident in every Plautine play that the Elizabethans must have been very familiar with it, and have frequently constructed it at the universities and other places for the performance of Latin comedies. Moreover, they wrote a number of plays for this identical form of stage: *Ralph Roister Doister* was written for a stage representing a street before the house of Dame Constance; *Gammer Gurton's Needle*, a street before the houses of Dame Chat and Gammer Gurton; *Jack Juggler*, a street before the house of Master Bongrace.

Many "probabilities" have been put forth to prove that the regular theaters differed as to the main parts of their stages, but no unquestionable facts. On the other hand, we have definite proof that certain ones were alike: the Hope theater was to be "made in all thinges and in suche forme and fashion as the said playhouse called the Swan"[1]; the stage of the Fortune theater was to be "contryved and fashioned like

---

[1] *Contract for Building the Hope Theater*.   Repr. G. P. Baker, *Development of Shakespeare as a Dramatist*, Appendix.

unto the stadge of the saide Playhouse called the Globe."[1]
The manner of play-writing at the time necessitated a similarity in the stages. Dramatists were then, as now, writing for
the highest market, and unless the stages of the different
theaters were one in principle, this would not have been
possible. The leading dramatic critic of to-day says, "A
play is destined for performance in a theater, and a practical
playwright can no more disregard the actual structure of his
stage than a composer can disregard the range and quality of
the instrument for which he is writing."[2] And lastly, the
majority of Elizabethan plays demand one form of stage.
There is virtually no distinction as to theater, as long as the
theater is one of the regular playhouses; and virtually no
distinction as to time, as long as the time is between, let us say,
1585 and 1642. It is impossible to prove this last point in a
limited space, but one illustration may be given: The Jew in
the *Jew of Malta* being one of Edward Alleyn's famous parts, the
play must have been frequently given at the Rose and the Theater; it was revived in the reign of Charles II at the Cockpit, and
printed in 1633. Thus the play was played in both public
and private theaters throughout a good part of the period.
However much the play may have suffered after it left the
hands of its author, the printed edition of 1633 demands the
same stage as plays published in the last decade of the sixteenth century. In fact, all the evidence that I am aware of
indicates that there was the same form of stage in all the regular theaters from the time of Marlowe to that of Shirley.
With this condition, I repeat, a study of a typical Shaksperian stage and the principles of Shaksperian play-production has nothing to do with particular dates and theaters.

In presenting the study I have attempted to give the
results of my investigation in a continuous and uninterrupted
form. For this reason I have carefully avoided constant
references to other studies of the stage and criticisms of their

---

[1] *Contract for Building the First Fortune Theater.* Repr. G. P. Baker,
Development of Shakespeare as a Dramatist, Appendix.

[2] William Archer, "The Elizabethan Stage", *Quarterly Review*,
April, 1908

interpretations. The three most thorough studies—*Die Shakespeare-Bühne nach den alten Bühnenanweisungen* by Cecil Brodmeier, *Some Principles of Elizabethan Staging* by G. F. Reynolds, and *Die Bühneneinrichtung des Shakespeareschen Theaters nach den zeitgenössischen Dramen* by Richard Wegener—have been reviewed in the Appendix. A complete list of the shorter articles on the stage has been included in the Bibliography.

Perhaps a brief outline of the essay at this point may be helpful. No complete summary of each chapter is here intended; the object is simply to outline in a more or less general way the main trend of the argument in the dissertation.

CHAPTER I. MIRACLES AND LONGER MORALITIES. In its infancy the religious drama was played on and between *sedes* or *domus* set at intervals down the choir and nave of a church. When it passed into the hands of the laity in their market-places and guild-halls, it was produced in either a stationary or a processional manner; that is, some plays were performed on and between stationary *sedes* arranged in a circle or some convenient form, while others were given on and around pageant wagons which moved through the city in one grand procession. In general, the *sedes* and pageant wagons contained settings and the *plateae* none; and in accordance with this arrangement, some scenes were written for a set stage and others for a bare one. A scene that required localization usually had a definite *sedes*, and an effort was always made to keep the action in congruity with the properties around it.

CHAPTER II. INTERLUDES AND SHORTER MORALITIES. The interludes and shorter moralities may be divided according to their staging into two general classes,—those needing properties in the action, and those requiring only a bare stage. As the performance was usually confined to a single scaffold and no front curtain was used, the author in writing his play chose either a propertied or an unpropertied stage—a *sedes* or a *platea*—for its production, and constructed his piece accordingly. If the play opened with a room, it closed with a room; if it opened with a street, it closed with a street; and in either case the action was usually in keeping with the setting.

CHAPTER III. A TYPICAL SHAKSPERIAN STAGE. First, the old drawings, usually known as the Swan, Red Bull, Roxana, and Messallina, are considered. Of the four, the last two are accepted as the most reliable. Next, the Restoration stage, as shown in the cuts in Settle's *Empress of Morocco*, is examined, and points of similarity between it and the stage shown in the Messallina picture are noted. With the ideas thus obtained Henslowe's *Contract for Building the First Fortune Theater* is compared to see in what way it supports and opposes them. Last, representative plays are studied, with an effort to determine the different features of the stage that are there repeatedly called for. In the end it is fairly well established that the typical Shaksperian stage contained the following parts: an outer and an inner stage separated by a curtain, two proscenium doors, a gallery closed by a curtain, two balcony windows, and a "hut." The approximate arrangement of these parts is shown in the Frontispiece.

CHAPTER IV. SOME PRINCIPLES OF RESTORATION STAGING. In the first place, a brief description of a modern melodrama is given as an introduction to the study of seventeenth-century staging. In the second place a few principles and special features of Restoration staging are considered for the light they throw on earlier conditions. In the typical Restoration play the action was continuous throughout the act; that is, no time was lost between the scenes. This principle of the continuous act was made possible by the facts that (1) the regular settings were on the inner stage; (2) the outer stage was usually bare; (3) when the curtains or "flats" were closed the outer space was a stage in itself, suited for all unpropertied action; (4) when the curtains or "flats" were drawn, the properties in the rear gave the whole space the appearance of being set, and the action took place over any part of the two stages. One of the ways of manipulating this duplex stage so as to secure continuity of action throughout the act was the alternation of outer and inner scenes. There were two special features in Restoration staging, which were undoubtedly survivals from Elizabethan times; namely, the use of the curtains or "flats" as doors to a house or room, and the change of scene with characters on the stage. This last feature has been blindly called by some writers on the Elizabethan stage "split scenes." No such term is needed, as the operation is nothing more than a change of scene without clearing the stage.

CHAPTERS V–VI. SHAKSPERIAN METHOD OF STAGE PRESENTATION. This question is discussed under the heads of principles and special features. To take up the principles first: 1. The properties of a regular setting were located on the inner stage, and changed for a new scene either during an act division or during the playing of a scene on the outer stage. There were special settings on the outer stage; frequently a few unimportant properties stood there throughout the play; and occasionally a simple, regular setting was placed there; but as a rule the settings were placed on the inner stage, and brought on and removed behind closed curtains. 2. When the curtains were closed, the space before them was a stage in itself; when the curtains were drawn, the outer and inner stages became one. The outer stage was the main scene of action, and the inner with its properties was used principally to mark the location and to give the appearance of a change of scene. 3. The action in an act was virtually continuous from the beginning to the end. This continuity of action was secured in three ways: (1) by the immediate succession of outer scenes; (2) by the succession of like-propertied inner scenes without a change of setting; (3) by the alternation of outer and inner scenes. It should be carefully noted that this last law is the principle of the *continuous act*, not that of the alternation of scenes. The dramatist endeavored—not always successfully, of course—to avoid delays between the scenes, and one of the means at his disposal was the alternation of outer and inner scenes. There is not, to my knowledge, a single play in which there is a complete alternation of scenes in every act; and, indeed, there are plays in which there is little or no alternation. The special features of Shaksperian staging which I have noted are the following: 1. Special settings.

Besides the regular settings there were special ones, which were placed on the outer stage and removed in full view of the audience. Two of these are a setting for a play within a play and a setting for a scene of execution. 2. Properties moved forward and new ones added. Among these are (1) small properties moved forward and added according to orders, (2) banquets brought on and removed, (3) beds carried on and moved forward.

I am perfectly aware that the discussion of the Shaksperian method of staging under the head of hard and fast principles is a very unsatisfactory way to treat the subject. No one would suppose that Shakspere had a set of principles of play-production in mind in writing his plays. He wrote them according to the established method of stage presentation of the day. That method changed slightly from time to time, and varied somewhat with different theaters and different plays. No set of principles will apply with equal force to all plays, or explain the exact conditions of every performance. But a search for differences and peculiarities cannot be expected to improve the vague and unsettled condition in which the problems of Shaksperian staging have long remained. I have, therefore, labored to condense the heterogeneous material into a few principles, hoping that the loss in accuracy will be more than compensated by the gain in clearness.

CHAPTER I

MIRACLES AND LONGER MORALITIES

Mr. E. K. Chambers has given us in *The Mediaeval Stage*[1] a careful and complete history of the English religious drama. At various places throughout his two volumes, he has discussed in some detail the material stage. Little of real importance remains to be added to his treatment of the actual mechanism of performance; but for the purpose of showing clearly the stage conditions in which the forefathers of the Elizabethans were schooled, a more collected as well as a more amplified study of the method of presenting these early plays may be given.

"One must," says Mr. Chambers, "conceive, I think, of the performances as gradually spreading from choir to nave, with the *domus, loca,* or *sedes* set at intervals against the pillars, while people crowded to watch in the aisles."[2] In connection with his conjectural stage plan of *The Resurrection* (See Plate 1-A) he further remarks: "And I would point out that such a scheme is simply a continuation of the arrangement down the choir and nave of a church suggested above. The crucifix is where it should stand in the church, above the altar.   The place of the monument corresponds to that most usual for the *sepulchrum,* on the north side of the chancel. The positions of heaven and hell are those in the former of stairs up to the rood-loft, in the latter of the stairs down to the crypt; and what, in a church, should serve for hell and heaven but crypt and rood-loft?   The Galilee answers to the porch at the west end of the church, which we know to

---

[1] E. K. Chambers, *The Mediaeval Stage,* 2 vols.   London, 1903.
[2] *Ibid.,* vol. ii, p. 79.

have been so called; and the castle of Emmaus stands in the middle of the nave, just as it did in the Fleury *Peregrini*. With my conjectural plan may be compared this actual plan of a sixteenth-century stage from Donaueschingen [See Plate I–B], in which a similar principle is apparent, the three divisions formed by cross-barriers corresponding to the three divisions of a church—sanctuary, choir, nave."[1]

This conclusion of Mr. Chambers, illustrated by the two drawings which I have reproduced in Plate I, shows that the English drama in its very infancy was staged in a systematic manner. For every localized scene there was an appropriate *sedes* on which to play it. The scenes of heaven had their Ciel *sedes;* those of hell, their Enfer *sedes*. Nicodemus had a special *domus;* so had Pilate, and Caiphas. There was a *sedes* for the sepulcher, another for the jail, and so on. Hell, heaven, the jail, the sepulcher, etc., were not all incongruously crowded on the same scaffold—that is, when the heaven scene, for example, was ended, its scaffold did not immediately become hell, and in turn Galilee, the jail, the sepulcher, the home of Nicodemus, and all the rest—but each scene that required localization had its own stage. In the large cathedrals sufficient space existed between the different *sedes* to keep each *domus* and its scene distinct from the others; and to allow certain parts of the action, such as the journeying from one house to another, to take place in the *plateae*. These *sedes* were probably raised platforms.[2] Some had perhaps few or no properties, and were there mainly to localize the scene; while others may have been fairly well propertied. In support of this last statement, notice the opening stage direction of the *Adam*, a twelfth- or thirteenth-century play: "A Paradise is to be made in a raised spot, with curtains and

----

[1] *Mediaeval Stage*, vol. ii, pp. 83, 84.

[2] See a reproduction of the miniatures in the MS. of the Valenciennes Passion in J. J. Jusserand, *Shakespeare in France*, p. 63; and in Petit de Julleville, *Histoire de la langue et de la littérature françaises*, vol. ii, p. 416; or, better still, a model of the Valenciennes stage in the Library of the Paris Opéra, and a duplicate of the same in the Library of Columbia University

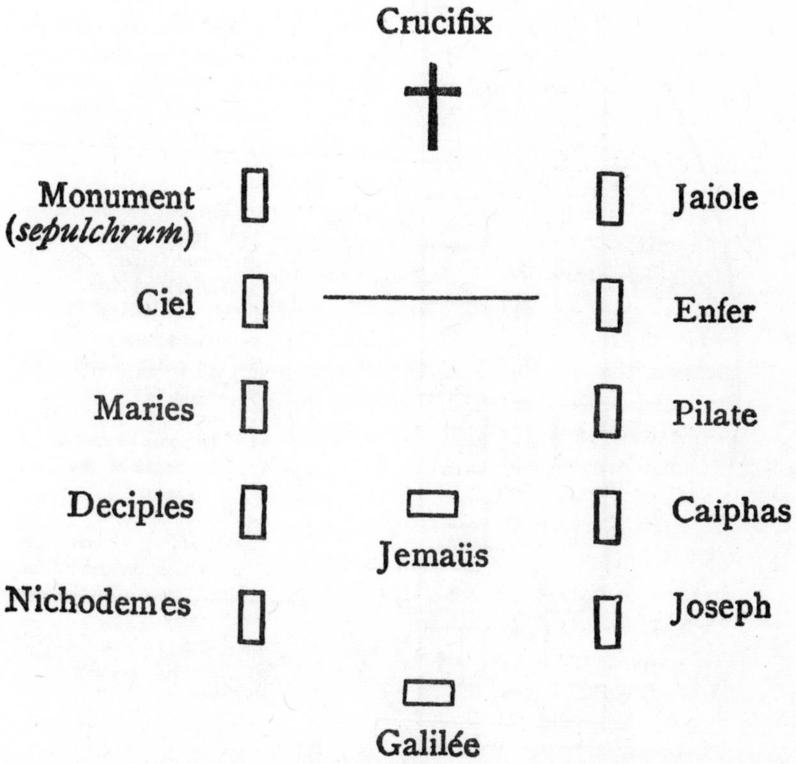

PLATE 1-A.—CHAMBER'S CONJECTURAL PLAN OF THE ANGLO-NORMAN *Ressurrection Play* STAGE IN A CHURCH IN THE TWELFTH CENTURY

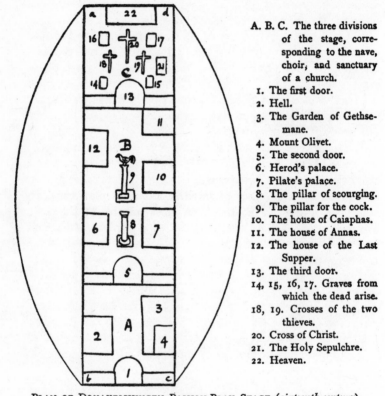

A. B. C. The three divisions of the stage, corresponding to the nave, choir, and sanctuary of a church.
1. The first door.
2. Hell.
3. The Garden of Gethsemane.
4. Mount Olivet.
5. The second door.
6. Herod's palace.
7. Pilate's palace.
8. The pillar of scourging.
9. The pillar for the cock.
10. The house of Caiaphas.
11. The house of Annas.
12. The house of the Last Supper.
13. The third door.
14, 15, 16, 17. Graves from which the dead arise.
18, 19. Crosses of the two thieves.
20. Cross of Christ.
21. The Holy Sepulchre.
22. Heaven.

PLAN OF DONAUESCHINGEN PASSION-PLAY STAGE (*sixteenth century*).

PLATE I–B.—PLAN OF DONAUESCHINGEN PASSION-PLAY STAGE IN A CHURCH IN THE SIXTEENTH CENTURY

cloths of silk hung round it at such a height that persons in the Paradise may be visible from the shoulders upwards. Fragrant flowers and leaves are to be set round about, and divers trees put therein with hanging fruit, so as to give the likeness of a most delicate spot." [1]

"Out of the hands of the clergy in their naves and choirs, it [the liturgic play] passed to those of the laity in their market-places and guild halls." [2]   Did the same general method of staging still continue?   Did the floor of the church with its *sedes* and *plateae* simply become the green of the town-square? Only a careful study of the miracles and longer moralities will answer these questions.

For the purpose of discussing the method of performance, the miracles and longer moralities may be divided into two classes,—stationary and processional.[3]   The stationary play was given on a number of fixed or movable platforms, arranged in a circle or in the form most suitable to the play. The processional play was produced on a number of pageant wagons which moved in procession through the town, each halting long enough at the appointed stations to allow the performance of its scene.   Had we the plans of all the early stages and the text of all the plays, it would be advisable to study the presentation of the plays of the two classes in chronological order; but as this is not the case, it seems more practicable to begin in each class with the plays about whose staging we are fairly sure, and from these to pass to analogous ones.

I. STATIONARY PLAYS

On the first leaf of the Macro MS., which dates from the reign of Edward IV, is a diagram of the stage of *The Castle of Perseverance*.   This stage plan and the descriptive matter

---

[1] *Mediaeval Stage,* vol. ii, p. 80

[2] *Ibid.,* p. 69.

[3] Mr. Chambers does not make a formal division into these two classes, but whenever he has an occasion to speak of the staging, he usually refers to it as "stationary" or "processional."

round about it give us an excellent idea of the method of staging a stationary play. For the sake of study and comparison, I reproduce in Plate 2 both the fac-simile and the modernized form of this diagram as it is given in the Early English Text edition of the *Macro Plays*.[1] The stage is arranged in the form of a circle, perhaps one hundred feet in diameter, encircled by a ditch or bar of some kind: "This is the water about the place, if any ditch may be made where (ther) it shall be played, or else that it be strongly barred all about; and let not over many auditors (stytelerys) be within the place." In the center is a rude representation of the castle: "This is the Castle of Perseverance, that standeth in the midst of the place; but let no men sit there, for letting of the sight; for there shall be the best of all." Between the pillars of the castle is an object intended for a bed: "Mankind's bed shall be under the Castle, and there shall the soul lie under the bed till he shall rise and play." A cupboard and most likely other properties were on the same stage: "Covetise's cupboard shall be at the end of the Castle, by the bed's feet." Around the outside are the names of the five scaffolds, which of course stood just within the ditch: "South, Caro scaffold—West, Mundus scaffold—North, Belial scaffold—North-east, Covetise scaffold—East, Deus scaffold."

From this it would appear that the castle was a fairly elaborate structure, all open underneath, with or without curtains, and was propertied with a bed, cupboard, and doubtless other things, which stood on a raised floor. The scaffolds were arranged around this central stage, and contained stools or whatever properties the scenes thereon called for. In fact, the stage plan is practically the same as that found in the church. The different characters had their homes on one or other of the *sedes;* and all the propertied scenes took place on or before these stages, while the unlocated ones, such as the traveling scenes, were acted on the *plateae* between the *sedes.* The audience sat or stood without the ditch, where they could see and hear, all that took place within the circle.

[1] *Macro Plays*, edited by F. J. Furnivall and A. W. Pollard for the E. E. T. S. Extra Series. Volume XCI.

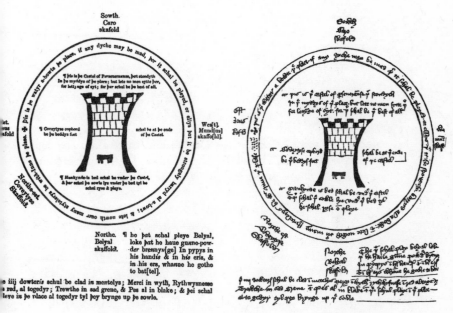

Sowth.
Caro
skafold

¶ his is þe Castel of Perseveranus, þet stondyth.
In þe myddys of þe place; but lete no men sytte þer,
for lettyage of syt; for þer schal be best of all.

West.
Mund[us]
skaffo[ld].

¶ Coveytyse cophord
be þe beddys fuet

schal be at þe ende
of þe Castel.

¶ Mankynde-is bed schal be vnder þe Castel,
& þer schal þe sowle lye vnder þe bed tyl he
schal ryse & pleye.

Northe.
Belyal
skafold.

¶ ho þat schal pleye Belyal,
loke þat he haue gunno-pow-
der brennyn[ge] In pypys in
his handis & in his eris, &
in his ers, whanne ho gothe
to bat[tel].

e iiij dowteris schul be clad in mentelys; Merci in wyth, Rythwysnesse
a red, al togedyr; Trewthe in sad grene, & Pes al in blake; & þei schal
leve in þe place al togedyr tyl þey brynge vp þe sowle.

PLATE 2.—STAGE PLAN OF *The Castle of Perseverance* (1461-1483)

Mary Magdalene[1] in the Digby MS. of about 1480–90 shows, in general, the same plan of staging. Following the scheme of the foregoing, I have ventured to give a plan of the complex and interesting stage for the play (Plate 3–A). In the center stands the castle of Maudleyn, and around it in a circle with a radius of about seventy-five feet are the eleven scaffolds or stations. "A-bowte the place," as in the *Castle of Perseverance*, "is the watyr, if any dyche may be mad," on which the shipman sails his boat, passing the home of Marcylle and on to the Holy Land. With a diagram of the stage before us, a brief outline of this rare, old miracle-morality play will show us how the different stages had their special scenes, and how the action passed from one *sedes* to another without delay of time, confusion of location, or incongruity of setting.

SCENE 1.[2] The audience is called to attention by Caesar arrogantly demanding silence. After giving his soldiers orders to keep a strict lookout for all Christians, the Emperor sits down to wine and spice.

SCENE 2. Cyrus, in the castle of Maudleyn, calls his children around him and divides his property among them; after this they, likewise, sit down to wine and spice.

SCENE 3. Caesar now directs his messenger to carry orders to Herod to search out all rebels and Christians,— "Here goth the masenger to-ward herowdes."

SCENES 4–5. Herod is busily engaged with his philosophers in looking up the records about that new Prophet when the news arrives. The *nuntius* delivers his letters, and is sent on to Pilate.

SCENE 6. Pilate, like Herod, gladly consents to the wishes of the Emperor, and dismisses the messenger with a reward.

SCENE 7. Cyrus dies, and Mary, Martha, and Lazarus are left alone in the castle.

SCENES 8–13. The World, the Flesh, and the Devil are now heard from their respective scaffolds. The Devil, "in a stage and Helle ondyr-neth that stage," is much perplexed

---

[1] *The Digby Plays*, edited by F. J. Furnivall for the E. E. T. S.   Extra Series, Volume LXX.

[2] The division into scenes is mine.

about Mary, and goes with his train to consult the King of the World. To this council on the World's *domus*, the King of the Flesh is summoned, and it is soon decided that Lechery with the bad angel shall tempt Mary while the six other deadly sins shall storm the castle.

SCENE 14. After a brief siege the conquest is won, and Mary, leaving her home to Martha and Lazarus, goes away with Lechery.

SCENE 15. On their way they enter a tavern where Mary falls in love with Curiosity, a dandy, and completes her downfall.

SCENE 16. The six devils here transfer their quarters to the house of Simon, while the bad angel returns to report the good news to his masters. The World, the Flesh, and the Devil, well pleased with the intelligence, immediately depart to their respective scaffolds.

SCENE 17. As Mary lies "asleep in the erbyr," she is shown the error of her way by the good angel, and awakes—

SCENES 18–20. To follow Christ and his disciples into Simon's house. Here she performs the well-known acts of kindness to Jesus, and becomes pure again.

SCENE 21. At Mary's conversion, the seven deadly sins rush back to Hell. The Devil rewards them for their idleness by giving them a sound trouncing and by burning the structure over Hell down on their heads.

SCENES 22–25. Next follows the Biblical story of Lazarus' death, burial, and resurrection.

SCENE 26. The characters on the scaffold of Marcylle now take part in the action. After considerable mock preparation, the King and Queen go to their little temple and offer sacrifice to Mahomet.

SCENES 27–30. Jesus has been crucified and buried, and these four scenes carry through the story from his resurrection to his appointment to meet his disciples in Galilee.

SCENES 31–33. Pilate, well content with his sentence, orders his messenger to make the rounds of Herod's and Caesar's scaffolds to report the glad tidings of the Traitor's death.

SCENES 34–35. As Mary enters, talking of the disciples

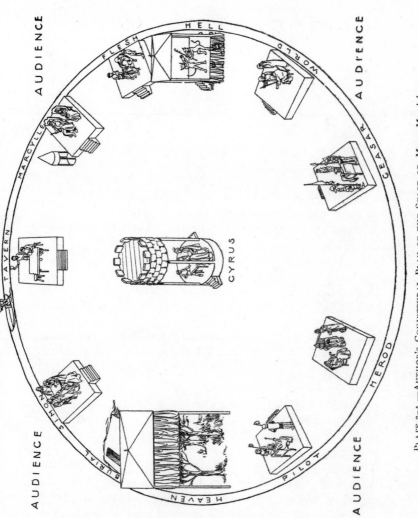

PLATE 3-A.—AUTHOR'S CONJECTURAL PLAN OF THE STAGE OF *Mary Magdalene*
IN THE FIFTEENTH CENTURY

now preaching in many lands, "hevyne xall opyne," and Jesus sends his angel to "tell Mary to go to Marcylle, convert the land, and become an Apostoless."

SCENE 36. Mary willingly consents, and a ship, now appearing, conveys her to the scene of her work.

SCENE 37. There she succeeds in converting the King and Queen. Leaving Mary in charge of the home, the royal converts set sail for the Holy Land to be baptized by Peter.

SCENE 38. On the way the Queen dies in child-birth, and is cast on a rock with her little one; the King, however, continues his journey, receives baptism, and sails homeward.

SCENE 39. When he nears the rock, the Queen awakes as from a sleep, and with the child in her arms passes with the King to the land of Marcylle.

SCENE 40. Mary has now accomplished her mission, and decides to spend the remainder of her life in prayer and fasting in the wilderness. There she is miraculously drawn up into the clouds each day and fed by the angels.

SCENE 41. At last Christ sends his angels to call her home; and after the priest has administered the sacrament, she dies and her soul returns to its maker.

This outline of the play, in connection with the diagram, makes it evident that every scene had a fairly definite place for its performance, and a more methodical, as well as a more realistic, presentation could hardly be desired. Though the staging is simple when once explained, yet there is considerable "business": the structure over hell and the little temple of Marcylle are burned down; "Here xall hevyne opyne and Iesus xall shew hymself"; angels descend and ascend and Mary is drawn up into the clouds and fed; and the little boat plies its way between Marcylle and the Holy Land.

An interesting "miracle" play of the fifteenth century, *The Blessed Sacrament*,[1] seems to require the same stage scheme, but one on a much simpler scale. The "chyrche" was possibly located in the center, and the scaffolds of the Bishop, Aristorius, and Jonathas in the usual circle around it.

---

[1] J. M. Manly, *Pre-Shaksperean Drama*, vol. i.

2

Jonathas "goo don of his stage" to "walke to see Arystories halle"; and when the Priest hears of his coming, he hastens "to hange your parlowr with pall." After Jonathas has bargained for the Host, Aristorius goes to the church, steals the Sacrament from the altar, and brings it to Jonathas, who has his servants spread the table and place it thereon. In the midst of the serious trouble with the miraculous "cake," they send for the Bishop, and "here shalle the bysshope enter into the Jewys howse." All matters are explained, and as they are marching to the church, Aristorius and the Priest see them and follow: "Here shall the merchant & hys prest go to the chyrche, & the bysshop shalle entre the chyrche & lay the Ost upon the auter."

To illustrate the stationary method of staging the long biblical cycles, we turn first to Cornwall. *The Ancient Cornish Drama*,[1] of the fourteenth century, consists of three groups of plays under the following names: *The Beginning of the World*, *The Passion of Our Lord Jesus Christ*, and *The Resurrection of Our Lord Jesus Christ*. The closing words of the first two groups show that the three dramas were intended to be played on three consecutive days. Along with each group in the MS. is a diagram of the stage used in that section of the cycle. There are eight *sedes* in each plan, and there is the usual circle-arrangement of the scaffolds.

The remains of two old Cornish theaters, or rounds, at St. Just and Perranzabulo, the former with stone and the latter with turf benches, are perfectly adapted to the stages shown in these diagrams. The earthen one has a "level area of 130 feet in diameter; this is surrounded by a continued earthen mound, 8 feet high, having seven turf benches on the inside; the top of the mound or rampart is 7 feet in width." In the area is a circular pit, 13 feet in diameter and 7 feet in depth, which leads by a channel 4½ feet wide to a semi-circular breach in the benches. The St. Just round is very much like the one at Perranzabulo, except that its tiers of seats are made of stone.

[1] *The Ancient Cornish Drama*, edited and translated by Edwin Norris, 2 vols., Oxford, 1859.

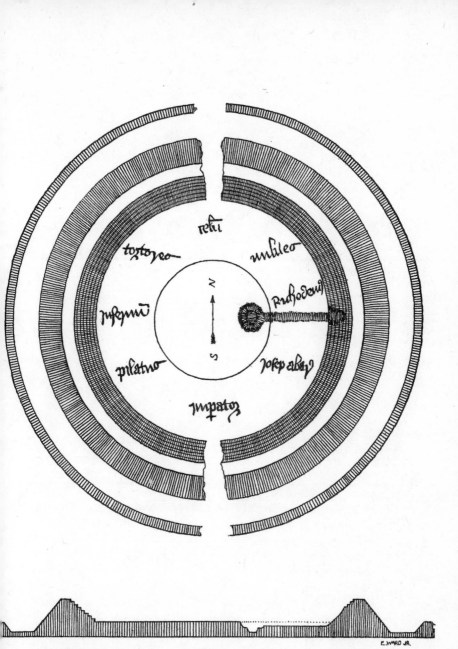

PLATE 3-B.—CORNISH THEATER AT PERRANZABULO IN THE FOURTEENTH CENTURY

Plate 3–B shows how perfectly the stage plans are adapted to the old rounds.   The diagram of the third group, *The Resurrection of Our Lord Jesus Christ,*[1] is here placed in the center of a drawing of the round at Perranzabulo.[2]   As there was frequent ascending and descending at Celum, this was likely the most elaborate stage; allowing, therefore, 30 feet per diameter or square for this *sedes* and 15 feet for each of the others, there would remain a space of about 32 feet one way and 85 the other between each *sedes* which would be amply sufficient to keep the locations distinct.   As in *The Castle of Perseverance*, the propertied and located action took place on and around the *sedes*, and the unpropertied and unlocated on the *plateae;* and as the action progressed from one scaffold to another, the audience, seated on the tiers of seats, could follow the scenes with all ease.

Ludus Coventriae[3] must be discussed in connection with the stationary plays.   This collection forms a complete cycle, but, as Ten Brink says, it is of a "composite character."   To show how part of it, at least, was given in the manner of the stationary play, I shall give a section of the cycle, starting where the play of "last year" left off and "we wold procede this year."

Two doctors speak the Prologue, "what tyme that processyon is enteryd into the place, and the Herowdys takyn his schaffalde, and Pylat and Annas and Cayphas here schaffaldys."   After the Expositor has introduced the play of the new year, "Herowndys xal shewe hymself and speke," ordering his soldiers to look well that no Christians, especially Jesus, escape his judgment.   A messenger, at this point, rushes "into the place," and hails Annas and Cayphas with the glad tidings that Christ is taken; "Here bryng thei Jhesus beforn Annas and Cayphas."   After insolent questioning and brutal torturing, they decide that they must have Pilate's word in order to put Jesus to death; so the messenger goes to

---

[1] *The Ancient Cornish Drama*, ed. and tr. by Edwin Norris, p. 200.

[2] T. C. Peter, *The Old Cornish Drama*, p. 45.

[3] *Ludus Coventriae*, edited by J. O. Halliwell for the Shakespeare Society, 1841.

Pilate, "who syttyth in his skaffald and the massanger knelyth to hym, thus seying:

> "My lord busshop Cayphas comawndyd hym to the,
> And prayd the to be at the mot-halle by the day dawe."

Pilate answers, "I xal be there in hast."

In the meantime, they have led "Jhesu abowt the place tyl thei come to the halle." Pilate can find no fault with him, and so the Jews, with the bishops, "take Jhehu and lede hym in gret hast to the Herowde; and the Herowdys scafald xal unclose, shewyng Herowdes in astat." Another series of insults and tortures follows, after which Christ is again commended to Pilate for judgment.

"Here enteryth Satan into the place in the most orryble wyse, and qwyl that he pleyth, thei xal don on Jhesus clothis . . . and ledyn hym abowth the place, and than to Pylat, be the tyme that hese wyf hath pleyd." Satan is exulting over the fact that Christ will soon be among his number, when "xal a devyl spekyn in helle":

> "Out upon thel we conjure the,
> That nevyr in helle we may hym se,
> Ffor and he onys in helle be,
> He xal oure power brest."

Satan now decides to use Pilate's wife as a means to keep Jesus alive: "Here xal the devyl gon to Pylatys wyf, the corteyn drawyn as she lyth in bedde; and he xal no dene make; but she xal sone after that he is come in, makyn a rewly noyse, commyng and rennyng of the schaffald, and her shert and her kyrtyl in here hand, and sche xal come beforn Pylat leke a mad woman seyng thus,

> "Pylat, I charge the that thou take hedel
> Deme not Jhesu, but be his frende!"

He consoles her:

> "Now to your chawm er ye do sewe,
> And alle xal be weyl, dame, as ye xal se."

"Here the Jewys bryng Jhesus agen to Pylat." He does
not wish to convict him, but at the unanimous cry, "crucify
him! crucify him!" "Pylat takyth Jhesu, and ledyth hym
into the cowncel hous." The fatal sentence is soon given;
and "Pylat xal rysyn and gon to his schaffald . . . ; and
the Jewys xul crye for joy with a gret voys, and arryn hym and
pu!lyn of his clothis, and byndyn hym to a pelere, and skorgyn
hym." "And qwhan he is skorgyd, thei put upon hym a
cloth of sylk, and settyn hym on a stol, and puttyn a kroune
of thornys on hese hed with forkys; and the Jewys knelyng to
Cryst, takyng hym a septer and skornyng hym, and than thei
xal pullyn of the purpyl clothe, and don on ageyn his owyn
clothis; and leyn the crosse on hese necke to berynt, and
drawyn hym forth with ropys; and than xal come to women
wepyng, and with here handes wryngyn."

When they have reached Gethsemane, "Than xul thei
pulle Jhesu out of his clothis, and leyn them togedyr; and ther
thei xul pullyn hym down and leyn along on the cros, and after
that naylyn hym thereon." When the cross is raised with the
thieves on either side, Mary comes weeping for Jesus and
"halse the crosse." "Here thei xal take oure lady from
the crosse, and here xal Pylat come down from his shaffald
with Cayphas and Annas, and alle here mené." The bishops
scorn the Saviour, and Pilate orders a tablet placed over his
head, bearing the inscription, "Hic est Jhesus Nazarenus rex
Judaeorum." "And so forth alle thei xal gon agen to the
skaffald." So on the action continues through the usual
cyclic events but this is sufficient to show the presentation.

Thus far it is evident that eight scaffolds were used at
various times throughout the action. The mot-hall or council
house was in the center: "Here the buschopys with here
clerks and the Phariseus mett, and the myd place, and ther xal
be a lytil oratory with stolys and cusshonys clenly be-seyn,
lyche as it were a cownsel-hous"; and around this in some
form were arranged the various scaffolds.

Several other features should be noticed in passing.
Some of the scaffolds were closed at times by curtains:
"Here xal Annas shewyn hymself in his stage—In the

mene tyme Cayphas shewyth himself in his skafhald arayed lyche to Annas—In the mene tyme the cownsel-hous beforn-seyd xal sodeynly onclose, schewyng the bus-chopys, prestys, and jewgys syttyng in here astat, lyche as it were a convocacyon—Here xal the devyl gon to Pylatys wyf, the corteyn drawyn as she lyth in bedde." Certain scaffolds were fairly well propertied: "Here Jhesus and his discipules go toward the mount of Olvyet; and whan he comyth a lytyl ther besyde, in a place lyche to a park, he byddyt his dyscipules abyde hym ther—and ther xal be a lytil oratory with stolys and cusshonys clenly be-seyn, lyche as it were a cownsel-hous." As to the rich robes worn, one quotation must suffice: "Here xal Annas shewyn hymself in his stage, be seyn after a busshop of the hoold lawe, in a skarlet gowne, and over that a blew tabbard furryd with whyte, and a mytere on his hed, after the hoold lawe; ii. doctorys stondyng by hym in furryd hodys, and on beforn hem with his staff of astat, and eche of hem on here hedys a furryd cappe, with a gret knop in the crowne, and on stondyng beforn as a Sarazyn, the wiche xal be his masangere."

The preceding analysis serves to show that at least part of the *Ludus Coventriae* was in a manner a stationary performance with the action taking place on and between scaffolds ar-ranged in a group. There is no reason to suppose, however, that the scaffolds were not regular pageant wagons. Each craft may have owned one of the pageant scaffolds and have supplied it with actors; and the main difference between this and a regular processional play would be that the companies here came in groups, and instead of each one giving a separate play, they all joined in the general play. These "theaters upon wheels" could have moved in groups from one "eminent part of the city to another," and have given a complete representation of the assigned yearly part at each of the three or four halting places.

Accounts in various town records show that the stationary play was of frequent occurrence throughout England during the Mediaeval period. "A play 'of the holy martyr St. George' was held in a field at Bassingbourne on the feast of St. Mar-

garet, July 20, 1511."[1] One of the items of expense was "for
setting up the stages."[1] "In 1564 the Corporation [of Lincoln]
ordered 'that a standing play of some story of the Bible
shall be played two days this summertime.' The subject
chosen was Tobias, and the place the Broadgate."[2] From
1495 on, the plays at Shrewsbury seem to have been given in a
"quary outside the walls."[3] There were a number of stationary plays at Skinners Well, London: "Vicesimo nono die
Augusti [1384] clerici Londoniae apud Skynnereswelle fecerunt
quendam ludum valde sumptuosum, duravitque quinque
diebus." "Item xviii° die Iulii [1391] clerici Londonienses
fecerunt ludum satis curiosum apud Skynnereswell per dies
quatuor duraturum, in quo tam vetus quam novum testamen-
tum oculariter ludendo monstrabant."[4] "This yere [1409]
was the play at Skynners Welle, whiche endured Wednesday,
Thorsday, Friday, and on Soneday it was ended."[5] "This
yeare [1409] was a great play at Skinners well neare unto
Clerkenwell, besides London, which lasted eight days, &
was of matter from the creation of the world."[6] "This year
[1411] beganne a gret pley from begynnyng of the worlde at the
skynners' welle, that lastyd vii dayes contynually; and there
ware the moste parte of the lordes and gentylles of Ynglond."[7]

II. PROCESSIONAL PLAYS.

The term "processional play" calls to our minds at once
the great York, Chester, and Towneley cycles. That these
complete cycles were ever played just as they now appear in the
MSS. is extremely doubtful. "The Chester texts are late
transcripts due to the zeal of local antiquaries, perhaps in
view of some frustrated revival."[8] "Some notes, probably
written when the plays were submitted to the Dean of York in
1579, state that xii, xvii, xviii, xxi [of the York Cycle] had

---

[1] *Mediaeval Stage*, vol. ii, p. 338.   [2] *Ibid.*, p. 379.
[3] *Ibid.*, p. 394.
[4] *Ibid.*, p. 380. [5] *Ibid.*, p. 380. [6] Stow, *Survey of London.*
[7] *Mediaeval Stage*, vol. ii, p. 381.   [8] *Ibid.*, p. 143.

been rewritten since the register was compiled."[1] The Towneley Plays, according to Pollard, were composed by three separate hands during a period of half a century. But regardless of these conditions, the great majority of the plays in these cycles were evidently intended for production in a continuous procession.

An idea of the method of presenting a processional cycle may be obtained from *A Breauarye of the Cittie of Chester*, "collected by the Reverend: mr. Robert Rogers," and "written by his sonne David Rogers" (1609): "The maner of these playes were, every company had his pagiant, which pagiante weare a high scafold with 2 rowmes, a higher and a lower, upon 4 wheeles. In the lower they apparelled themselves, and in the higher rowme they played, beinge all open on tope, that all behollders might heare and see them. The places where they played them was in every streete. They began first at the Abay gates, and when the first pagiante was played, it was wheeled to the highe crosse before the Mayor, and so to every streete, and soe every streete had a pagiante playing before them at one time, till all the paigantes for the daye appointed weare played, and when one pagiant was neere ended, worde was broughte from streete to streete, that soe they might come in place thereof, exceedinge orderly, and all the streetes have their pagiants afore them all at one time playeinge togeather; to see which playes was great resorte; and also scafolds and stages made in the streetes in those places where they determined to play theire pagiantes." From this description we can picture to ourselves one of those spectacular processions,—a long train of pageant wagons slowly moving through the town, and each halting long enough to produce its special scene at "the Abay gates," at "the highe crosse before the Mayor," and at the other appointed places.

The method of staging in the processional play is, indeed, very much like that in the stationary. As Mr. Chambers says, "it [the pageant wagon] is simply the raised *locus*, *sedes*, or *domus* of the stationary play put upon wheels."[2]

---

[1] *Mediaeval Stage*, vol. ii, p. 412.   [2] *Ibid.*, p. 138.

In the stage of *The Castle of Perseverance* the scaffolds are arranged in a circle; each scaffold represents a distinct location throughout the play, while the *plateae* between the *sedes* are common property and serve for all unlocated and unpropertied scenes. In the York Plays, for example, this circle of scaffolds is straightened out into a long train; each pageant wagon is propertied to represent one, or, where the scenes are very much alike, two locations; and a certain proportion of the action takes place in the street around the carriage: "Here Erode ragis in the pagond and in the strete also."

There are, however, certain plays in the cycles which require two or three distinct locations with characters traveling from one location to another. We can conceive of a very spacious wagon with two or three raised platforms on it, and the characters making a circle out in the street when they are supposed to pass from one place to another; or we can conceive of certain actors taking their stand in the street as though they were on raised platforms, and passing from these spots to and from the pageant wagon as the action requires. But there is some evidence of another and a far more reasonable way. The quotation from Rogers ends with the sentence, "And also scafolds and stages [were] made in the streetes in those places where they determined to play theire pagiantes." Mr. Sharp, while searching "the ancient Books and Documents belonging to the Corporation [of Coventry], and the remaining Account Books and other writings of the Trading Companies," was constantly meeting with items for extra scaffolds on wheels, and eventually came to the following conclusion: "Various charges in the Pageant Accounts demonstrate that at Coventry, as at Chester, it was customary to have scaffolds or stages for the accommodation of the spectators: a few instances will suffice:—making of a new post to the scaffold;—a tryndyll and a theal to ditto;—two new scaffold wheels 6s. 8d.;—iron pins and colters to the scaffold wheels;—boards about the scaffold;—three boards and a ledge for the scaffold;—clamps and iron works;—setting in of the Pageant and scaffolds;—driving the Pageant and scaffolds. From these items it is evident that the 'scaffolds' were placed upon wheels, and moved with the Pageant, to which it probably was attached, as the usual charges are for 'having out of the Pageant, setting in the scaffolds: and setting in of the Pageant and scaffolds' to the Pageant-house after the performance was over."[1]

But Mr. Sharp's conclusion on this subject did not seem practical even to himself when he came to represent his ideas in a drawing. In planning his elaborate Frontispiece, he decided that "the situation afforded such ample room for the numerous spectators" that it was "judged advisable not to introduce any representation of the movable scaffolds." And why was this situation different from any other? As in France, seats may have been erected in the streets, though I know of no place where they are called stages; but a seating apparatus was certainly not pulled along with each one of these heavy four- and six-wheeled pageants. The untold inconvenience that would arise to the honored occupants every time one pageant moved into a station and another out is perhaps the least objection to such an arrangement.

A more useful and necessary place for these inconspicuous scaffolds, inconspicuous both in the processions and in the accounts of the guilds, would be in the staging-apparatus. One or two of these "stages" could accompany the pageant that was playing a double- or treble-scene play, and could be used in the performance in the same way as the scaffolds around the castle in *The Castle of Perseverance*. In this way a difficulty would be removed in the staging of some of the more complex plays in the processional cycles.

The majority of the plays in the York cycle, many of those in the Chester and Towneley, and perhaps all in the Norwich can be given on single wagons, but certain plays in the first three cycles require more than one platform to keep the locations of the different scenes clearly distinguished. It is noticed in these double- and triple-scene plays that there is one spectacular scene (or two, where the scenes are very similar)

[1] T. Sharp, *Dissertation on the Pageants or Dramatic Mysteries anciently performed at Coventry*, p. 20.

demanding special properties, and one or two accompanying scenes which need few or no properties, but which are too definitely located to be played in the street.

My idea, therefore, is that the pageant wagons sufficed in some of the plays in the processional cycles, while in others, one or two plain scaffolds with few or no properties accompanied each pageant carriage. [1]   In certain cities, as at Coventry, these scaffolds were placed on wheels and drawn along with the pageants that needed them; in others, as at Chester, they were "made in the streetes in those places where they determined to play theire pagiantes."   In both cases they were arranged at a distance of fifty to seventy-five feet from the main carriage.   The spectacular scene took place on the pageant wagon, and the unscenic one or two on the scaffold or scaffolds near by; and the characters passed freely from one to the other, doing part of the acting on the *plateae*, just as in the stationary play.

An analysis of some of the plays which have more than one episode in them may be given in conclusion:

York, Abraham and Isaac.   God hears the prayer of Abraham and demands the sacrifice (scaffold).   Abraham and Isaac make ready, and ride to the foot of the mountain, where they leave their asses in charge of the servants and ascend to the sacrifice (pageant).

York, The Angels and the Shepherds.   The shepherds have met and are in the midst of a discussion (scaffold), when the star appears and directs them to the place where Christ is born (pageant).

York, The Entry into Jerusalem.   Christ, after talking with his disciples (scaffold), mounts an ass and rides to the city (pageant), blessing the people on the way.

Towneley, First Shepherds' Play.   The shepherds eat their frugal meal, and then indulge in a general wrestling match (scaffold).   After this the Star of Bethlehem appears and directs them to the holy manger (pageant).

---

[1] There were no doubt some whole cycles, now lost, in which the single pageant wagon for each play was all that was needed or used.

Towneley, Purification. Simeon praying that he may see the Christ and die (one scaffold) is directed to the temple, where the bells are ringing (pageant). Mary and Joseph (on another scaffold) think it time for the purification, and start for the temple. There (at the pageant) they are all supposed to meet.

Chester, Passion of Christ. Christ is sent from the Bishops (one scaffold) to Pilate (on the pageant wagon, because most of the action takes place there), who in turn sends him to Herod (another scaffold). He is soon returned to Pilate (pageant), where the trial, final judgment, and long scenes of torture follow.

Looking back over the whole field of the miracles and longer moralities, we find that the religious drama was staged in its birthplace on and between *sedes* arranged in a regular order along the sanctuary, choir, and nave. One branch from this parent stock continued in the open air practically the same form of staging which it had used in the church; the other branch placed the old *sedes* on wheels and gave its plays successively in a processional manner. A very noticeable feature of the staging throughout is the attempt to keep the locations of the different scenes distinct; each scene that is localized or uses particular properties has its own scaffold, and its ground is not intruded on by a differently propertied scene. Much of the staging of this early drama seems to us crude and somewhat incongruous, but a complete survey of the whole shows that its general aim, and often its attainment, was a method of staging surprisingly regular, consistent, and congruous for the age in which it was produced.

CHAPTER II

INTERLUDES AND SHORTER MORALITIES

WHILE the old pageants were rolling on their rounds in the distant cities less and less frequently, a new form of drama was springing up largely in and about London. A more portable as well as a more adaptable form of amusement was taking their place. The courts, the universities, and the general public were beginning to demand plays not once a year, but as often as they found leisure and remuneration for the actors. The plays could no longer command a large open space—a field, a cathedral, or a "round"—but must be given on a single scaffold at one end of a hall, at some cross, or in an inn-yard.

From the usual idea of Elizabethan staging,[1] we should expect the most incongruous presentation at this early period of the drama and stage, but investigation reveals quite the contrary. We have seen that in the miracle plays propertied and located action took place on definite *sedes*, whose settings were always in keeping with the action on them; and that unlocated action usually occurred on the *plateae* between the *domus*. When the drama was confined to one scaffold, no attempt was made to change the old-time principles of staging; the new play and the new stage were made to conform to *them*.

Any grouping of this heterogeneous mass of plays before 1570, here termed interludes and shorter moralities, must clip the corners of many, but some such a classification seems

---

[1] Cf. G. F. Reynolds, *Some Principles of Elizabethan Staging, Modern Philology*, April and June, 1905; "*Trees" on the Stage of Shakspeare, ibid.*, October, 1907; and my discussion of these articles, infra, pp. 152–160.

advisable for a discussion of their staging. Roughly, they may be grouped as follows: 1. Plays in which the action is entirely unlocated and requires no properties; that is, the action takes place on neutral ground in the great somewhere, and no properties, such as tables, chairs, trees, etc., are needed. 2. Plays with located and propertied action. The stage for this class is set before the play opens with the properties necessary for the action, and is not cleared and re-set during the performance. 3. Plays in which the scenes are unlocated and require only such properties as can stand wherever needed. 4. Plays in which the scenes are located in or near some building, but in which no properties are mentioned and in most cases not needed. In listing the plays under these heads, first an outline of a representative play in each group will be given by way of illustration; the most difficult rather than the most typical one will be selected out of each class.

I. PLAYS IN WHICH THE ACTION IS ENTIRELY UNLOCATED AND REQUIRES NO STATIONARY PROPERTIES IN THE REPRESENTATION

Respublica, ACT I, SCENE 1.[1] After the prologue has been recited, Avarice enters, contemplating how he may enrich himself on Lady Respublica; but suddenly remembering his unlocked chests, he hastens home.

SCENE 2. Adulation, Insolence, Oppression appear; the last two soon persuade the first that he should be a great man and "rule the roast" (roost).

SCENES 3–4. Avarice returns—all is safe at home—and the four form a league to assail Lady Respublica. All assume praiseworthy names and exeunt for business.

ACT II, SCENE 1. Respublica enters, lamenting the serious condition of her commonwealth,—

SCENE 2.—and is soon joined by Avarice, now called Policy. He has come to her rescue, but in order fully to assist her, he

---

[1] The division into acts and scenes is according to the sixteenth-century MS. of the play.

must have the coöperation of his friends, Honesty, Reformation, and Authority. He goes out,—

Scene 3.—and presently returns with his helpmates; a league of pretended aid is formed.

Act III, Scene 1. Enter Respublica. She thinks all is going well—

Scene 2.—and is very much encouraged by Adulation, who simply overflows with praises for his companions and their noble work.

Scene 3. Here People appears with considerable muttering, but is soon hushed and sent away to hope for the future; Respublica, also, goes off in contentment.

Scene 4. In comes Avarice dragging his bags of gold, and heartily greets Adulation.

Scenes 5–6. Oppression soon joins them, and later Insolence. After each has told how admirably he has succeeded, all hasten off, trusting in the goddess, Occasion.

Act IV, Scene 1. Respublica comes in, wondering why her commonwealth does not improve, and presently—

Scene 2.—People appears on the scene, saying that "he mends as sour ale in summer, that is, still worse and worse."

Scenes 3–4. Avarice, Oppression, and Insolence are at hand to save their cause, and soon succeed in sending the lady away "to hope a while longer." People, now at their mercy, is shamefully treated, and warned never to complain again to his "Rice-pudding-cake" (Respublica). All exeunt.

Act V, Scene 1. Misercordia appears, sent from God in behalf of the commonwealth;—

Scene 2.—and is welcomed by the sad and distressed Respublica.

Scene 3. Vertus is summoned, and the villains who have been sucking the life blood from the country are at once revealed.

Scene 4. Justice and Peace presently join them to assist in redressing the wrongs of Respublica, and all go off singing, to clothe her anew.

Scene 5. The "advisers" fear their doom has come, but

Adulation hastens out to collect his companions while Avarice remains to see what he can do with Respublica.

SCENE 6.   Respublica enters with the "nymphs bearing up her train," and tells Avarice to be gone.

SCENE 7.   With the greatest timidity People advances, but to his surprise finds a hearty welcome; times have changed, and he has a new coat and "in his purse a silver groat."

SCENES 8-10.   The villains are tried before the "virtues," and proper punishment is allotted to each by Nemesis. And with a prayer for Queen Mary, the Council, and the Commonwealth, the play closes.

Here is a play with all the dignity of acts and scenes, and yet the greatest care has been taken by the author to have the characters meet on neutral ground, so that the interlude could be played anywhere and at any time. Lady Respublica goes from here to "wink" and to dress, Insolence "goes home," Oppression "abroad," Avarice to see "what feet about my door have trod"; but the place in which they meet in the play is never mentioned, nor are any stationary properties needed.

The following are staged in much the same manner: *Wit and Science, Lusty Juventus, The Four Ps, God's Promises, New Custom, Impatient Poverty, Wealth and Health, Play of Love, Mind, Will, and Understanding, Disobedient Child, Trial of Treasure, Magnificence, Albion Knight.*

II.   PLAYS WITH LOCATED AND PROPERTIED ACTION

Thersites.   Thersites introduces himself as the fellow about whom all have read in Homer, and proceeds to boast of his great might and bravery. Turning at length to Mulciber's shop, located in the rear, he calls for a sallet. After considerable delay, he is fitted out with a new armor by the smith, and steps forward, challenging all the old heroes of romance to meet him in open fight. His first opponent is a snail, which he assaults vigorously, and after a terrible battle, compels to draw in its horns. Miles has entered during the combat, and as Thersites turns around to exult in his victory, a new adversary faces him; he loses his courage in a trice, and takes refuge behind his mother "in her place."   A letter is now brought from Ulysses, which requests the old woman to cure Telemachus of worms by her magic spells, and to accompany him home to dinner with her son.   After pronouncing a terrible curse on the worms which fully cures Telemachus, she goes within to dress for the party.   While she is away, Thersites falls to boasting again,—he would kill even his mother; but at this juncture Miles appears, and so frightens the braggart that he drops his club and sword and flees.

In this interlude the stage was completely arranged before the play opened, and remained unchanged during the performance; and every episode was in perfect keeping with this setting.   Nor was the stage-setting so simple: "Mulciber must have a shop made in the place and Thersites cometh before it"; "And then he goeth into his shop and maketh a sallet for him."   There was a special place prepared for the mother: "Then the mother goeth into the place prepared for her."   A snail came in and eventually drew in its horns; and the armor and sword of Thersites were made in Mulciber's shop.

With this play may be classed the following: *King Darius* (a banquet is served in the council-chamber and removed), *Mankind* (an open-air play beside a tree), *Marriage of Wit and Science*, *Queen Hester*, *The Summoning of Everyman*, *Play of the Weather*, *Johan Johan*, *Tyb*, and *Jhon* (the priest is called from a door at some other part of the room), *Kynge Johan*, *Mundus et Infans*, *Nature*.

III. PLAYS IN WHICH THE SCENES ARE UNLOCATED AND REQUIRE ONLY SUCH PROPERTIES AS CAN STAND ANYWHERE

Calisto and Meliboea.[1] SCENE 1.   Enter Meliboea.   She is soliloquizing on fond and foolish lovers,—

SCENE 2.—when Calisto appears and pleads his love to her; but is spurned.   Exit Meliboea.

SCENE 3.   Sempronio, a parasite, now joins Calisto.   The

---

[1] I have for convenience divided this play into six scenes.

3

lover prays the parasite, "Go fet me my lute, and bring some chair or stool with thee, the argument of love I may dispute." Sempronio obeys, and the dispute of love takes place; at the close the parasite promises aid and goes for old Celestina, the bawd, "while Calisto will go walk in his orchard."

SCENE 4. Celestina enters, relating some of the experiences she has had with her girls. She is looking for Sempronio, who "for me about doth inquire, and it was told me I should find him here." Calisto soon appears with his accomplices, but is reminded at once by the bawd that "words are but wind, for money maketh the merchant." He hastens off, and returns in a short time with "an hundred pieces of gold"; at the receipt of this, Celestina assures him that she will "bring it about even as ye would."

SCENE 5. Celestina and Meliboea meet, and after a long argument in which the bawd thinks she has accomplished her purpose, the two part, Meliboea going to her home and the other to Calisto.

SCENE 6. Danio, Meliboea's father, is wandering about in a great quandary over his recent dream, when he finds his daughter and proceeds at once to tell her all about it: There seemed to be two baths, one wholesome and pleasant and the other vile and polluted. Meliboea was walking towards the pure one, but a "foul, rough bitch" enticed her to the very brink of the other. Just as she was about to fall in, he awoke from his slumbers. Meliboea recognizes at once the significance of the dream, and falling on her knees before her father, confesses her own temptation and prays to "God for grace all vice to eschew." The father points the moral of the play, as usual, and they depart.

The stage in this play is a common meeting place, but never once localized; and so careful is the author about congruity that not even a stool is on the stage, but one is brought on for the occasion and doubtless removed when no longer needed. The following plays are in a great measure like this: *Cambises* (containing a banquet, which is set here just for the occasion, "meaning in this place repast to take," and later "to the court to return"), *Nice Wanton, Appius and Virginia* (a coffin is brought on the scene. "Here let Virginius go about the scaffold" means that he is to walk around on the stage, just as we speak of a man walking about the house), *Like Will to Like, Hycke-Scorner.*

IV. PLAYS IN WHICH THE SCENES ARE LOCATED IN OR NEAR
    SOME BUILDING, BUT IN WHICH NO PROPERTIES ARE
    MENTIONED AND IN MOST CASES NOT NEEDED

There are still a few other plays, which scarcely form a class and yet have in common the one characteristic of being located in or near some building. The scene in *John the Evangelist* represents the interior of a cathedral, where some are walking and others are listening to a sermon. This could be presented on a very small stage with perhaps a pulpit and a curtained space for a tiring room. *The Interlude of Youth* and *The Four Elements* have no definite locations, but both are supposed to be played near a tavern; in the first the characters in action hear a riot in a neighboring tavern, and in the second one of the doors represents an entrance to an inn.

While no special effort has been made to classify all the extant interludes, the majority of those accessible to students has been included in the foregoing groups. To enumerate them again according to their classes: I. *Wit and Science, Lusty Juventus, The Four Ps, God's Promises, New Custom, Impatient Poverty, Wealth and Health, Play of Love, Mind, Will, and Understanding, Respublica, Disobedient Child, Trial of Treasure, Magnificence, Albion Knight.* II. *King Darius, Mankind, The Marriage of Wit and Science, Queen Hester, The Summoning of Everyman, Play of the Weather, Johan Johan, Tyb, and Jhon, Kynge Johan, Mundus et Infans, Nature, Thersites.* III. *Calisto and Meliboea, Cambises, Nice Wanton, Appius and Virginia, Like Will to Like, Hycke-Scorner.* IV. *John the Evangelist, The Interlude of Youth, The Four Elements.* This classification cannot be exact, but it shows very clearly the general principles on which the dramatists staged their plays. It would be hard to conceive of any period of a hundred years producing a cruder lot of plays, partly experimental, partly following the older religious drama, varying in subject, treatment, and merit; in fact, there is only one principle which seems to underlie all, a principle not always observed but far oftener than we might at first suppose,—that of consistency in staging.

In the main, all these plays according to their staging fall into two classes, propertied and unpropertied; the first being usually definitely located because of its setting, the second unlocated except for its occasional connection with some building. A play once started in either of these classes seldom breaks over into the other: if it opens with the characters on neutral ground, it closes in the same way; if it opens with a definite setting, it keeps that setting throughout and the action and characters are so arranged as to be always in harmony with their little stage world. Nothing is more noticeable than the constant effort put forth to hold to this principle; the characters describe many important scenes in houses, taverns, woods, etc., all of which are crying to come on the stage, but the sanctity of the one-scene stage allows the audience to have only an echo of the elsewhere.

This was a time when incongruity in staging was really needed. Throughout the greater part of the history of the early English drama, the typical play contained from a few to many propertied scenes; now it must be confined to one propertied scene. How convenient and advantageous it would have been in these interludes for an actor to say as he appeared on the stage, I am now in a dense forest, now on a battle-field, and now in the palace of the king! This, however, the extant interludes show never to have existed to any great extent. A bare stage could represent a bare spot anywhere on the earth, and could be in whatever place, town, or country the actor located it with his lines; but a propertied stage had to be the same throughout, not necessarily confined to one place but distinctly to one kind of place,[1] and

[1] It might be a court in England at one time and the same in Scotland at another, but never, as a rule, a room one moment and a forest the next.

the characters had to belong there regularly or make their
excuse for so appearing.

Therefore the method of staging in the interludes was only
a repetition of that learned in the miracles and longer moralities.   There could not be here a change from one scaffold to
another with a vast deal of action between them; the whole
stage was no larger than one of the old pageant wagons.   It
could, therefore, represent either a *sedes* or a *platea*, but not
both.   To these two alternatives the dramatists were confined, and to these two they did confine themselves; they
wrote their plays either for a *sedes* or for a *platea*.   The fact
that they labored through a long period of time under such
limitations shows that the principle of congruity was firmly
established on the English stage centuries before the first
permanent theater was built.

Before passing from the early English drama to the Shaksperian, we may state the conclusions which we have reached
from our study of the staging of the miracles, moralities, and
interludes: 1. There were two kinds of scenes,—those
requiring properties in the action and therefore usually localized, and those requiring no properties in the action and
consequently often unlocalized.   2.   The action was generally
in keeping with the stationary properties.   When the time
came to confine the story drama to a single platform within
the walls of the Theater and Curtain, it was necessary to
devise a stage on which both propertied and unpropertied
scenes could be given in rapid succession with the action still
congruous with the stationary properties.   And this, as we
shall see in the next chapter, was devised.

CHAPTER III

A TYPICAL SHAKSPERIAN STAGE

THE OUTER-INNER STAGE

ALL the regular theaters of the Elizabethan period,[1] but one, were opened during the lifetime of Shakspere: The Theater and Curtain in 1576-7; Rose, 1592; Swan, 1594; Blackfriars, 1596; Globe, 1599; Fortune, 1601; Red Bull, 1608; Hope, 1613; Cockpit, 1616; Salisbury Court, 1629. The Red Bull, Cockpit, and Salisbury Court survived the Commonwealth, and were used at the opening of the Restoration. Despite De Witt's statement that the Swan "is built of flint, ... and as to shape seems to be an imitation of Roman work," these old playhouses have entirely disappeared, and no remains are left to be studied and cherished. The stage, however, of this period still lives in the Elizabethan plays: they were written expressly for that stage, and must contain an impression of at least its main parts. One play may show one part, another another, and only a consistent examination of many plays will give a picture of the whole. Such an examination is directed as well as restrained by authentic pictures, contemporary statements, fundamental principles of dramatic art, and the form of the Restoration stage,—the successor and perhaps the direct outgrowth of the Elizabethan.

There exist four pictures which have usually passed as illustrations of the Shaksperian stage: the drawing by Van Buchell of the Swan stage; the sketch prefixed to Kirkman's editions of *The Wits, or Sport upon Sport*, generally known

---

[1] Elizabethan is used throughout this study for the entire period, 1576-1648.

38

by the title "Inside the Red Bull Playhouse"; and those
found in the frontispieces to the editions of the tragedies of
Roxana and *Messallina*. (For the sake of brevity these
prints and the stages there represented will always be referred to as the Swan, Red Bull, Roxana, and Messallina.)
A glance at the four cuts will show both similarity
and dissimilarity in their stages: the Red Bull and Swan
differ from each other and also from the last two, while the
Roxana and Messallina are practically alike. The Swan has
two large doors at the rear and no curtain, the Red Bull one
door at the rear closed by a curtain, the Roxana and Messallina a curtain extending across the entire visible rear of the
outer stage,—a space not less than twenty feet. These conditions, alone, if the pictures are all genuine, make it impossible
to establish a typical stage of the period. Therefore, a searching inquiry must first be made as to the origin of these plates.

Mr. W. J. Lawrence, in an article in *Englische Studien*, vol.
32,[1] has stated succinctly about all the definite proof that
can be collected against the Swan picture. The headings of
his argument are as follows: "1. It is at best but 'hearsay
evidence,' being a drawing of one Arend van Buchell from
the instructions of his friend Johannes de Witt. 2. It is
undated. 3. It is self-contradictory. 4. It affords no in-
dication of the upper or lower traverses." The facts which
he has here clearly and concisely stated are strong evidences
against the German drawing. To his work I would add only
a few statements, or rather amplify what is there implied.
1. Many of the Elizabethan plays, conforming to a fundamental principle of acting, demand a straight passage across
the stage. Two doors close together on the same plane make
this impossible. 2. This picture shows no curtains, although
plays from Marlowe to Shirley call for a curtain. 3. Any
attempts to supply this stage with a curtain leads to two
difficulties: first, it makes a clumsy, awkward arrangement;
and second, it creates a stage entirely out of harmony with
any European or succeeding English stage.

[1] *Cf.* W. J. Lawrence, "Some Characteristics of the Elizabethan–
Stuart Stage," *Englische Studien*, vol. xxxii, pp. 44–48.

The truth about the plate seems to me to be this. It is a picture drawn on hearsay evidence by a man unacquainted with the art of acting, and, as a result, is impracticable, self-contradictory, and lacks some of the necessary parts; those which are here, however, as doors, gallery, "hut," etc., undoubtedly existed in the Elizabethan stage, but the exact location of these parts, as well as the supplying of those that are wanting, must be determined by other contemporary evidence.

The Red Bull picture forms the frontispieces to Francis Kirkman's editions of the Drolls, a collection of comic, one-act scenes played during the Commonwealth and published in the Restoration, under the title of *The Wits, or Sport upon Sport*,—Pt. I in 1672, Pt. II in 1673, and a collected edition of I and II later in 1673.[1] There is absolutely no title to the cuts, and the title-pages and prefaces state that these scenes were played "When the publique Theatres were shut up," "in London at Bartholomew Faire, in the Country at other Faires. In Halls and Taverns. On several Mountebancks Stages, at Charing-Cross, Lincoln-Inn-Fields, and other places. By several Stroleing Players, Fools, and Fidlers, and the Mountebancks Zanies."[2] In the Preface of Pt. II there is a passing remark about the chance performances in the Red Bull theater, and from this the name has been unauthoritatively applied to this crude little stage; and the picture is now published in books on the Elizabethan drama with the title, "Inside the Red Bull Playhouse."

A short review of the history of the closing of the theaters will show the state of the Red Bull stage during the Commonwealth. On September 12, 1642, an Ordinance[3] of the Lords and Commons was published which commanded "that while these sad causes and set times of humiliation do continue,

---

[1] An edition was published by Marsh in 1662, but, so far as is known, contained no drawings.

[2] Title-page of Part II.

[3] *Ordinance of both Houses of Parliament, for the suppressing of public stage playes throughout the kingdom during these calamitous times.* Repr. Collier's *English Dramatic Poetry*, vol. ii, p. 105.

publick stage-plays shall cease and be forborne." In 1647 the war was virtually at an end, and the theatrical world was again hopeful; but on July 17th the House of Parliament renewed the Ordinance, fixing its date of expiration at January 1, 1648. During the year an attempt was made to give Beaumont and Fletcher's play, *A King and No King*, but the sheriff immediately broke up the performance and arrested the leading actor. When January 1st came around, the playhouses promptly proceeded to open their doors. At the Fortune something like one hundred and twenty coaches set down their passengers; the Red Bull opened with Beaumont and Fletcher's *Wit without Money*, and the Cockpit with another of Beaumont and Fletcher's plays, *The Bloody Brother*. The last performance was cut short by the appearance of a squad of soldiers at the door, who arrested the actors and put them into temporary imprisonment.

Parliament was now thoroughly aroused, and on February 11, 1648, passed a final Ordinance: "And it is further ordered and ordained by the authority aforesaid, that the Lord Mayor, Justices of the Peace, and Sheriffs of the City of London and Westminster, and of the Counties of Middlesex and Surrey, or any two or more of them, shall and may and are hereby authorised and required to pull down and demolish, or cause or procure to be pulled down and demolished, all Stage Galleries, Seats and Boxes, erected or used, or which shall be erected and used, for the acting or playing, or being acted or played, such Stage-playes, etc."[1] Their object was to remove the temptation from the actors by making it utterly impossible to give a play, and therefore the insides of the theaters were completely stripped of all those appliances which were thought necessary to the production of a play, such as stage galleries, boxes, etc., and perhaps nothing but the bare walls were left standing. This was the condition of the Red Bull at the time of the Drolls.

That the picture first printed in 1672 had no connection with the Elizabethan stage is further proven by the fact that

---

[1] *Scobell's Collection of Acts & Ordinances*. The one here referred to is reprinted in Collier's *English Dramatic Poetry*, vol. ii, p. 114.

it shows only a bare platform with a curtain hung across the single door, while the Red Bull stage was the scene of some specially propertied plays, such as Heywood's *Ages*, with their forests, battle fields, council chambers, ascending and descending gods, large properties, large "discovered scenes," and a frequent call for "one door—the other door—several doors." Moreover, the print shows a stage with branches and rabbit-eared foot-lights, but the Red Bull needed no such artificial lighting. "The Globe, Fortune, and Red Bull were large houses and lay partly open to the weather, and they always acted by daylight."[1]

The solution of the matter is not difficult. These comic scenes or episodes, existing at a time when the stages in the regular theaters were torn down, were played on hastily improvised stages anywhere throughout the country. The ever present Puritan law forbade the actors to build a regular stage; and, more than this, a single platform was all that was needed for the Drolls. "Then all that we could divert ourselves with were these Humours and pieces of plays, which passing under the name of merry conceited Fellows called Bottom the Weaver, Simpleton the Smith, John Swabber, or some such title were only allowed us, and that by stealth too, and under pretense of rope dancing or the like. . . . 'Enter Red Coat and exit Hat and Cloak' was very true, not only in the Audience, but the Actors too were commonly not only stripped, but many times imprisoned."[2]

Kirkman is outspoken in his purpose: "Now I must tell you, my Plot with these Humorurs is clearly for sale; for I intend to raise no other Reputation to myself than that of ready money; and that I only bespeak in these preparatory Lines."[3] The collection seems to have been published largely for strolling companies and occasional entertainments, and the prefaces strongly recommend it for such use. "As for those Players who intend to wander and go a stroleing, this very Book, and a few ordinary properties is enough to set

[1] James Wright, *Historia Histrionica*. Repr. Hazlitt's *Dodsley*, vol. xiv.
[2] Preface to Part II.   [3] Preface to Part I.

them up, and get money in any Town in England. And Fiddlers purchasing of this Book have a sufficient stock for all Feasts and Entertainments. And if the Mountebancks will but carry the Book, and three or four young Fellows to Act what is here set down for them, it will most certainly draw in auditors enough, who must needs purchase their Drugs, Potions, and Balsoms. This Book is also of great use at Sea, as well as on Land, for the merry Saylors in long Voyages, to the East and West Indies." [1]

To further advertise the simplicity of the plays and the ease with which they could be given, he attaches the picture of a plain stage, real or imaginary, with some of his characters upon it. "Clause" is a leading figure in *The Lame Commonwealth*, [2] the "French Dancing Mr." in the *Humours of Monsieur Galliard*, [3] "Sr. I. Falstafe" and "Hostes" in *The Bouncing Knight*, [4] "Bubble," shouting "Tue quo que," in *The Bubble*, [5] and "Simpleton" in *Simpleton the Smith*, [6] in which rôle Robert Cox seems always to have made a "hit" when he appeared with a great piece of bread and butter, complaining "that a man cannot be left undisturbed to eat a little bit for his afternoon lunchin."

We may conclude, therefore, that this picture in no sense represents an Elizabethan stage, but a stage for the Drolls, and was published with Kirkman's editions of the Drolls largely for advertisement. Perhaps it was drawn partly from imagination and partly from the actual performance of plays on hastily constructed platforms for the nonce in the ruined theaters, private houses, halls, inn-yards, anywhere and at any time the law-defying actors could get a stand. [7]

The Roxana picture forms part of the frontispiece to the

---

[1] Preface to Part II.
[2] Taken from *The Beggars' Bush*.
[3] *The Variety.*
[4] *I Henry IV.*
[5] *Greene's Tu Quoque.*
[6] An independent farce.
[7] I have undertaken to edit *The Wits, or Sport upon Sport* from Kirkman's collected edition of 1673. This rare collection, besides being very interesting in itself, represents a distinct period in the English drama

Tragedy of Roxana.[1] The full title-page reads: "Roxana Tragaedia a plagiarii unguibus Vindicata, aucta, & agnita ab authore Gulielmo Alabastro. Londini, Excudebat Gulielmus Jones, 1632." "William Alabaster was born at Hadleigh, Suffolk; scholar of Westminster school; elected to Trinity, Cambridge, 1583; M.A. 'ad eundem' Oxford, July 7th, 1592; chaplain to Robert Earl of Essex in the Cadiz voyage, 1595; became a Roman Catholic, but returned to the Church of England; appointed prebendary of St. Paul's, D.D. and Rector of Tharfield, Hertfordshire. Died April, 1640."[2] The *Tragedy of Roxana* "was several times acted at Trinity, Cambridge."[2] The life of the author, the Latin language in which the play is written, and the place where it was acted, all indicate that it is a college play, and the stage on its frontispiece a college stage, perhaps that of Trinity.

The Messallina picture is found in the lower central part of the frontispiece to the *Tragedy of Messallina.* The title-page in full is as follows: "The Tragedy of Messallina, The Roman Empresse. As it hath beene Acted With generall applause divers times, by the Company of his Majesties Revells. Written by Nathanael Richards. 'Optimus hic & fomosissimus idem Gentis patritiae rapitur miser extinguendus. Messallinae oculis,' Iuvenal, Satyr. 10. London, Printed by Tho. Cotes for Daniel Frere, at the signe of the Red Bull in Little Brittains, 1640." The introductory verse by Tho. Rawlins "To his worthy Friend Mr. Nathanael Richards, upon his Tragedy of Messallina" ends with this couplet:

> "Applaud that happy wit whose veines can stirre
> Religious thoughts, though in a Theator."

The Prologue and Epilogue are impersonal in their appeal and have the tone of the regular public play. A couplet from the latter shows distinctly that the play was written for a theater:

[1] *Cf.* G. B. Churchill and W. Keller, "Die lateinischen Universitäts-Dramen in der Zeit der Konigen Elizabeth," *Shakespeare Jahrbuch,* vol. xxxiv, p. 252.
[2] F. G. Fleay, *Chronicle of the English Drama,* vol. i, p. 23.

PLATE 5.—FRONTISPIECE TO THE *Tragedy of Messallina*

" Why should we doubt?   This Theater do's appeare
The Musicke Rome of concord; you being here."

As already stated, it was acted by the Revels Company.
Among the list of actors opposite the *dramatis personae*
are Will Cartwright, who had been an actor at the Fortune,
and Christopher Good, a former member of the Queen's men.
Fleay states, "For the Revels Company acting at the Bull,
from 1635 to 1637, Rawlins and Richards wrote."[1]   Among
the plays of Richards, acted at the Red Bull by the Revels,
may have been the *Tragedy of Messallina*.

To sum up, the *Tragedy of Messallina* is an English play
published within the Elizabethan period, and "acted with
generall applause divers times, by the Company of his Majesties Revells," "in a Theator."   The Revels acted at different
theaters, among which was the Red Bull, where they gave
Richards's plays.   The picture on the frontispiece shows a
permanently constructed stage with a curtain under the
outer edge of the gallery and a solid railing around the outer
stage.   Strong evidences, therefore, point to the conclusion
that the Messallina is a picture of a regular Elizabethan
stage, and may be that of the Red Bull.

The result of our research on the four pictures stands as
follows: the Swan and Red Bull are fairly challenged, if not
completely disproved; the Roxana and Messallina may be
accepted as authentic pictures, the former showing a college
stage of the period and the latter a regular public Elizabethan
stage, perhaps that of the Red Bull.   (As these two stages
are one in principle, we shall regularly refer hereafter only to
the Messallina.)   The problem now remains to establish a
typical Elizabethan stage, first, by means of such proof as
may be collected outside of the plays, and second, by the aid
of the plays themselves.

Some evidence outside of the plays may be derived from a
study of the origin and form of the Restoration stage.   The

[1] F. G. Fleay, "The History of the Theatres in London from their
first opening in 1576 to their closing in 1642," *Royal Historical Society
Transactions*, vol. 10, p. 129.

theaters were partially closed in 1642, but not finally until February 11, 1648.   On May 26, 1656, an entertainment was given by Davenant in "the back part of the Rutland House," and, later in the year, the *Siege of Rhodes* at the same place. In 1658 Davenant produced at the Cockpit, *The Cruelties of the Spaniards in Peru,* and in 1659, *The History of Sir Francis Drake.* Before 1660 a second company had collected at the Red Bull, and a third began to act at Salisbury Court.   On August 21, 1660, Charles II issued a patent granting to Sir William Davenant and Thomas Killigrew the right of creating two companies of players.   Davenant began his work that year in Salisbury Court, but also continued to use the Cockpit; Killigrew opened with a new theater in Vere Street, Clare Market, November 8, 1660, but still retained the Red Bull under his management.   In 1662 Davenant moved to his new theater in Portugal Row,[1] but maintained the Cockpit and Salisbury Court for some time.   On January 15, 1662, a patent was granted to Davenant for a new theater, and on April 25th the same was granted to Killigrew.[2]   On April 8, 1663, at three o'clock, Killigrew opened the new Theater Royal in Drury Lane with the *Humorous Lieutenant,*[3] and November 9, 1671, Davenant's heirs opened the Duke's theater in Dorset Garden with *Sir Martin Mar-all.*[4]

The English theater, therefore, was closed about ten years, during which time the Drolls were being played here, there, and everywhere.   The Restoration drama opened in the old Elizabethan theaters,—Cockpit, Red Bull, and Salisbury Court.   Killigrew built at once, but Davenant continued for over a year in Salisbury Court and Cockpit.   These facts show that there was no great break between the two periods.   The stages themselves were torn down in 1648, and just how they were rebuilt at the opening can not be determined, though, from a remark by Davenant that the place for the scenery,

---

[1] *Cf.* John Downes, *Roscius Anglicanus.*
[2] *Cf.* Patents reprinted in Fitzgerald's *New History of the English Stage,* vol. i, pp. 73–80.
[3] *Cf.* play-bill for the opening day, Fitzgerald, vol. i, p. 87.
[4] *Cf.* John Downes, *Roscius Anglicanus.*

PLATE 6.—STAGE OF THE DUKE'S THEATER IN 1673

or "scenes," was only eleven feet high, it would seem that even the old gallery was again erected.

The first pictures that we have of a Restoration playhouse are those of the Duke's theater, built in 1671. They are found in the edition of Settle's *Empress of Morocco*. The full title page is: "The Empress of Morocco, a Tragedy. With Sculptures. As it is Acted at the Duke's Theatre. Written by Elkanah Settle, Servant to his Majesty. 'Primos da versibus annos.' Petr. Arb. London, Printed for William Cademan at the Popes-head in the Lower Walks of the New Exchange in the Strand, 1673." This publication contains one cut of the exterior and four of the stage, the last one of which is here reprinted for the purpose of study and comparison. (Plate 6.)

Now let us examine carefully the different parts of this stage. There is one scenic opening, perhaps 25 feet square, where the curtain plays back and forth; behind this is a stage of the same width and height as the scenic opening and from 15 to 25 feet in depth, on which are located all the properties, —this we will call the inner stage; before the curtain, the stage extends towards the audience to a considerable distance, even beyond the limits of the picture,—this we will term the outer stage; on either side of the outer stage is seen the edge of a door,—these two openings are usually known as the proscenium doors, as they are the regular entrances to the outer stage; and over either door is a large balcony window or door with a railing before it. Therefore, the Restoration stage contained five distinct parts,—inner stage and outer stage with a curtain between them, proscenium doors leading on to the outer stage, and balcony windows over the doors. The location of the properties will be considered in Chapter V, but we may note here, in passing, that the setting is all on the inner stage, and that the outer is entirely bare.

Comparing the Messallina with this picture, we find certain parts in common. There is an outer stage with a curtain, perhaps 25 feet wide, across the rear, and evidences of a space behind this curtain, which corresponds to the Restoration inner stage. The only real difference here, so far

as the Messallina is visible, lies in a gallery, which cuts
the inner stage horizontally into two stories, an upper and a
lower, each about 12 feet high, while in the Duke's this
partition is removed and all is one story, perhaps 25 feet in
height.

The picture of the Duke's stage is cut so close on either
side that it seems a mere chance that we are left a glimpse of
the proscenium doors. In the Messallina print the sides of
the stage, up even with the ends of the gallery, are covered
with the encroaching pictures of the "sheep" and the "goat."
That fair-sized corners of the outer stage are cut off is evident
from the railing,—only four posts are visible in the side
railing, which cannot possibly represent more than half of
the length of these diverging sides. Since the outer and
inner stage, separated by a curtain, tally in the two pictures,
we have every reason to believe that the corners of these
stages were also alike; that is, there was a proscenium door
on either side of the stage shown in the Messallina picture
just where it is found in the Duke's. If the Restoration did
not get the idea of the outer-inner stage with proscenium
doors from the Elizabethan stage, where did it come from?
The accompanying cut (Plate 7) of the stage of Richelieu,
opened January 14, 1641, shows a picture-frame stage. This
is what the English, seeking refuge in France during the Commonwealth, had before them, and certainly no one would think
of devising the duplex Restoration stage from this picture-
frame stage of Richelieu.   Is it not more reasonable to suppose
that it is simply a modified form of the old Elizabethan stage?
The outer stage and proscenium doors are one and inseparable.
To anticipate a little our discussion of the plays, what use
would there be of an outer stage without a means of entrance?
If characters entered through the curtains, then why have a
curtain?   An actor would certainly not walk out from behind
the curtain only to turn around and discover to himself some
object or person by drawing the curtain.

The warlike history of this combination—outer stage and
proscenium doors—through the next one hundred and fifty
years shows that it was not a temporary device, but deeply

PLATE 7.—STAGE OF RICHELIEU IN 1641

rooted in the very structure of the English drama.   In 1699
Christopher Rich slightly remodeled the old Drury Lane
theater, cutting away about four feet of the outer stage and
changing the location of the doors a little.   From this time
on the outer stage was gradually shortened and used less and
less as a place of action, but not till 1780 did Drury Lane attempt to take away the doors and put boxes in their places.
However, the need for the old arrangement was yet so great
that in a short time they were replaced.   In 1782 Covent
Garden followed the example of Drury Lane but was equally
unsuccessful, and in 1792 the doors were back again.   In 1793
Drury Lane made another attempt but failed.   In 1812 the
New Drury Lane theater was opened and the proscenium
doors were missing; but after trying the new arrangement for
a few seasons the historic doors were restored to their former
place.   In 1822 they were taken away from Drury Lane never
to return as permanent fixtures, and in 1823 Covent Garden
followed the same custom.

The inner stage during these one hundred and fifty years
gradually grew deeper and the outer stage shallower, until
finally both outer stage and proscenium doors disappeared.
They had not gone, however, but only passed within the
proscenium arch and were there temporarily constructed
whenever needed.   Even to-day they may occasionally be
seen in this disguised form.   The modern "drop," joined at
both ends by "wings" with doors in them, makes a structure
very similar to the outer stage and proscenium doors of three
hundred years ago.   Here the clog dancer finds his place
between the acts in vaudeville performances, and many a scene
in the cheaper melodramas is given on this new-old outer stage.

The Restoration stage and its succeeding history show both
the presence and persistence of the proscenium doors.   The
Messallina picture as it stands is wholly neutral, offering no
proof for or against doors.   There seems to be a prevailing
amount of evidence, therefore, in favor of supposing that on
both sides of the outer stage in the cut-off corners there were
proscenium doors, arranged much the same as we find them
in the Duke's theater.

4

Just over either proscenium door in the Duke's stage is an arched opening with a balustrade before it, which serves both for a balcony window and door.   Here again, the Messallina being neutral, and no precedent for such an arrangement in the French theaters, and no proof to the contrary, we may suppose that, in the Elizabethan stage, over the proscenium doors and on the same plane with the gallery, were balcony windows.

So far, there would be but one main difference between the Restoration and Elizabethan stage—namely, that of the gallery or two-storied inner stage.   While no proof exists, yet a reasonable explanation may be offered for the absence of this feature in the Duke's stage.   The English during their stay in France had learned the advantage of painted scenery or the "art of perspective in scenes," and on their return they would wish to introduce this into the English theaters.   The old gallery stood seriously in the way of this new element. Davenant seems to have chafed under its presence for some time, which shows that it was becoming a nuisance, and at least by 1673—the date of the pictures of the Duke's theater —it was gone, and the whole inner stage given up to one setting.   When old and new elements clash, the old usually go, and this seems to have been the fate of the gallery.

Before we sum up our conception of the stage from external proofs, let us notice that the figures of the *Contract for Building the First Fortune Theater*[1] in no way clash with our ideas, but on the contrary support them.   "The said howse to be sett square, and to conteine flowerscore foote of lawful assize everye waie square, without, and fiftie five foote of like assize square, every waie within; . . . and the saide frame to conteine three stories in height, the first or lower storie to conteine twelve foote of lawful assize in heighth, the second storie eleaven foote of lawful assize in heighth, and the third or upper storie to conteine nine foote of lawful assize in heighth.   All which stories shall conteine twelve foote and a half of lawful assize in breadth throughoute, besides a juttey forwards in eyther of

[1] Repr. G. P. Baker, *Development of Shakespeare as a Dramatist*, Appendix.

the saide two upper stories of tene ynches of lawful assize; . . .
with a stadge and tyreinge-howse, to be made, erected, and
sett upp within the saide frame; . . . and which stadge shall
conteine in length fortie and three foote of lawfull assize, and
in breadth to extende to the middle of the yards of the said
howse; and the same stadge to be paled in belowe with goode
stronge and sufficyent new oken boardes; . . . and the said
stadge to be in all other proportions contryved and fashioned like unto the stadge of the saide Play house called the
Globe."

If we are to infer from this that the second balcony extended
all the way around, and that the first was on a level with
the lower stage, it would make the stage gallery 13½ feet deep
and the inner stage 12 feet high.   These dimensions agree
very well with the apparent size of the gallery and inner stage
in the Messallina print.   Again the stage was to extend forth
into the pit and be "paled in," both of which features are
just what we find in the two authentic pictures of the Elizabethan stage.   From such inferences as we can gather from
all sources, independent of the plays, the following seems to
be the form of the Shaksperian stage: an outer stage, 20 to 30
feet deep and 20 to 25 feet wide at the curtain; a proscenium
door at either side of the same with a balcony window above
it; an inner stage at the rear 10 to 12 feet deep, 20 to 25 feet
wide, and 12 feet high, with a gallery of the same length and
breadth just over it; and a curtain 20 to 25 feet by 12 feet
playing between the outer and inner stage, and discovering
and closing the latter.

With this outline before us we will now turn to the plays
and seek to establish a typical stage.   Each part of the stage
will be taken up separately and illustrations given to prove
the use and necessity of the same.

I.   A FAIR-SIZED SPACE CLOSED BY A CURTAIN

Before attempting to locate the curtained space, we will
first show by giving a few stage directions from the quartos

and folios that such a space actually existed, and that it was of considerable size.

II Tamburlaine, II, 3. "The arras is drawen, and Zeno-crate lies in her bed of state, Tamburlaine sitting by her, three Phisitians about her bed tempering potions. Theri-damas, Techelles, Vsumcasane, and the three sonnes."

David and Bethsabe, I, 1. "He [the Prologue] drawes a curtaine and discovers Bethsabe, with her Maid, bathing over a spring."

Dido, I, 1. "Here the curtains draw:—there is discovered Jupiter dandling Ganymede upon his knee, and Mercury lying asleep."

Downfall of Robert Earl of Huntington, III, 2. "Curtain opens: Robin Hood sleeps on a green bank, and Marian strewing flowers on him "

Grim the Collier of Croydon, I, 1. "The curtains drawn on a sudden; Pluto, Minos, Aeacus, Rhadamanthus set in counsel; before them Malbecco's ghost guarded with furies."

Love's Sacrifice, V, 1. "Enter above Fiormodo. A cur-taine drawne, below are discovered Biancha, in her night attire, leaning on a cushion at a Table, holding Fernando by the hand."

Friar Bacon and Friar Bungay, IV, 1. "Enter Friar Bacon drawing the courtaines, with a white sticke, a booke in his hand, and a lampe lighted by him, and the brasen head and Miles, with weapons by him."

Insatiate Countess, I, 1. "The Countesse of Swevia dis-covered sitting at a table covered with blacke, on which stands two black tapers lighted, she in mourning."

Wisdom of Doctor Dodypoll, I, 1. "A Curtaine drawne, Earle Lassingbergh is discovered (like a Painter) painting Lucillia, who sits working on a piece of Cushion worke."

The Guardian, III, 8. "Enter Jolante (with a rich Banquet and Tapers) in a Chair behind a Curtain."

Martyred Soldier, III, 2. "Eugenius discovered sitting loaden with many Irons, a Lampe burning by him; then enter Clowne with a piece of browne bread and a Carret roote."

Satiro-mastix, I, 2. "Horrace sitting in a study behinde a Curtaine, a candle by him burning, bookes lying confusedly; to himselfe."

Whore of Babylon, Prologue. "He [the Prologue] drawes a Curtaine, discovering Truth in sad abiliments; uncrownd: her haire disheveld, & sleeping on a Rock: Time (her father) attired likewise in black, and al his properties (as Sithe, Howre-glasse and Wings) of the same Cullor, using all means to waken Truth, but not being able to doe it, he sits by her and mourns."

A Wife for a Month, III, 1. "Enter divers Monks, Alphonso going to the Tomb, Rugio and Frier Marco, discover the Tomb and a Chair."

Platonic Lovers, II, 1. "Draws a Canopy; Eurithea is found sleeping on a Couch, a Veil on, with her Lute."

I Iron Age, IV, 1. "Achilles discovered in his Tent, about him his bleeding Mermidons, himselfe wounded, and with him Vlisses."

Brazen Age, II, 2. "Two fiery Buls are discovered, the Fleece hanging over them, and the Dragon sleeping beneath them."

What You Will, II, 1. "Enter a Schole-maister, draws the curtains behind, with Battus, Nows, Slip, Nathaniell, and Holifernes Pippo, schole-boyes, sitting, with bookes in their hands."

Merry Beggars, I, 1. "He opens the scene; the Beggars are discovered in their postures; then they issue forth; and last, the Patricio."

Merry Beggars, II, 1. "Randal opens the Scene. The Beggars discovered at their Feast. After they have scrambled a while at their Victuals: This song."

These and many other illustrations that could be collected make a fair-sized curtained space, somewhere on the stage, imperative. Would an enclosure 25 feet by 10 be sufficient for all these discovered scenes? We must answer, yes. Then why may not this space, which we will hereafter call the inner stage, be located at the rear of the outer stage behind the curtain, as shown in the Messallina picture? This question must be answered in connection with the next section.[1]

II. AN OUTER STAGE APPROACHED BY TWO PROSCENIUM DOORS, AND AN INNER STAGE AT THE REAR SEPARATED FROM THE OUTER BY A CURTAIN

This can best be shown by cases where characters enter the outer stage, and, while there, the curtains are drawn, revealing to them some object or persons on the inner stage.

Looking Glass for London and England, II, 1. They have just closed the curtains to the Queen's chamber, according to her orders, when the King enters with the Magi. They perform tricks before him, and he passes off and on the stage; but finally he approaches the chamber of fair Remelia with the words, "Now ope, ye foldes." "He drawes the Curtaines and finds her stroken with Thunder, blacke." In this scene the outer stage with its entrance is used quite independently of the inner: the King, though he has passed off and on the stage during the exhibition, knows nothing of the fate of the Queen until the curtains are drawn.

First Part of the Contention, Scene 2. Duke Humphrey has been smothered in bed. Later the King enters and hears of his death. Warwick says: "Enter his privie chamber my lord and view the bodie. Good father staie you with the rude multitude, till I returne." "Exet Salisbury. Warwick drawes the curtaines and showes Duke Humphrey in his bed."

---

[1] The metaphorical use of the terms the "curtain's drawing," "open the scene," etc., should be noticed: it strongly suggests that the people were familiar with the practice of drawing a curtain on the stage.

Sejanus, III, 1. Tiberius has just obtained full sway over the senate and commands them to proceed to their affairs. Aruntius, knowing well that some trick is now at hand, remarks aside: "Now, Silius, guard thee; The curtain's drawing. Afer advanceth."

Monsieur Thomas, III, 1. A crowd of friends have come to rally Frank who is sick in bed, and have brought along some "old reverend Sack." As Thomas is about to take out the bottles, he says, "Sit thee down, Frank, and see what I have brought thee· come discover, open the Scene, and let the work appear."

The outer stage is here entered and used independently of
the inner, and some of the characters on the outer stage are
entirely ignorant of what is on the inner until the curtains
are drawn.

Downfall of Robert Earl of Huntington, III, 2.   "Enter
Fitzwater." After a soliloquy, the "Curtains open: Robin Hood
sleeps on a green bank, and Marian strewing flowers on him."
Again the outer stage is entered and used independently,
and later, the curtains drawn, the inner stage is discovered.

Edward I, Scene 10.   "King Edward, Edmund and Glocester goes into the Queen's chamber; the Queen's tent opens; she
is discovered in her bed, attended by Mary Duchess of Lancaster, Joan of Acon her daughter; and the Queen dandles
his young son." After a scene, "They close the tent," and
the King and lords welcome the Welch barons. The "mantle
of frieze" is accepted, the barons exeunt, and Edward hastens
to present the gift to the young Prince,—"The Queen's tent
opens; the King, his brother, the Earl of Glocester, enter."
The outer stage is entered and used independently of the
inner, and the actors on the two stages are unknown to each
other until the curtains are drawn.

Whore of Babylon, Prologue. After the Prologue has
spoken, "He drawes a Curtaine, discovering Truth in sad
abiliments; uncrowned; her haire disheveld, & sleeping on a
Rock: Time (her Father) attired likewise in black, and al his
properties (as Sithe, Howre-glasse and Wings) of the same
Cullor." Soon a funeral procession passes by and Truth
awakens. There is no direct statement that the procession
marched across the outer stage, entering one proscenium
door and passing out the other, but all is natural and easy this
way, and it is hard to conceive how else the scene could be
played effectively.

If this be not a good Play, the Devil is in it, V. "The play
ending, as they goe off, from under the ground in severall
places, rise up spirits, to them enter, leaping in great joy,
Rufman, Shackle-soule, and Lurchall, discovering behind a
curten, Ravillac, Guy Faulx, Bartervile, a Prodigall, standing
in their torments." Later in the scene "Curtaines are drawne

over them," and the action continues on the outer stage.
Here again the outer stage is entered and used independently
of the inner, and in course of the action the curtains are
opened and closed.

II Edward IV. "Enter at the one doore, Dighton, with
Edward under his arm, at the other doore, Forrest with
Richard." After a few remarks "They lay them down," and
exeunt, saying, "The priest here in the Tower will bury them.
Let us away." Here both proscenium doors are used, and,
while no mention is made of the curtain, it must have been
closed when the murderers left, as there is no other way provided for the mimic dead to escape.

King of Lombardy, V, 1. "A canopy is drawn, the king
is discover'd sleeping over Papers; Enter Paradine, with his
Sword drawn." He kills the King, and, hearing a knock at
the door, "puts him behind the Arras, opens the door. Enter
Rhodolinda." After she is similarly disposed of, "Enter Her-
megild, Thesina." In the course of the action, "He draws
the Arras, and discovers Alboyine, Rhodolinda, Valdaura,
dead in Chairs." The outer stage is entered and used independently of the inner, and the curtains opened and closed
at the pleasure of Paradine.

Henry VIII, II, 2. "Enter Lord Chamberlaine, reading
his Letter." Soon "Enter to the Lord Chamberlaine, the
Dukes of Norfolke and Suffolke." After a brief discussion of
Wolsey's influence on the King, "Exit Lord Chamberlaine,
and the King drawes the Curtaine and sits reading pensively."
The outer stage is entered and used independently of the inner
until the curtains are drawn and the King discovered.

Distresses, IV, 1. "Enter Leonte, and second Servant."
After a few instructions, he dismisses him, and "steps to the
Arras softly, draws it. Claramante is discovered sleeping on
her Book, her Glass by." Here the entrance of Leonte and his
servant is plainly through one of the proscenium doors to the
outer stage, from which place he draws the arras and discovers
the inner scene.

White Devil, V, 4. "Enter Flam and Gasp at one dore,
another way, Giovanni, attended." After several incidents

have taken place, Florence enters to tell Flamineo that his mother has grown wild with grief over her dead boy. Flamineo says: "I will see them. They are behind the travers. Ile discover their superstitious howling." "Cornelia, the Moore and 3. other Ladies discovered, winding Marcello's coarse. A song." There can be no doubt here that both proscenium doors were used as entrance to the outer stage, and not till well along in the action did the curtains draw revealing the inner stage.

Shop scenes may be mentioned here because they are so well adapted to the outer-inner stage. The shop or shops were likely ranged along just at the edge of the inner stage, so that they could be discovered and closed by the curtain, while the outer stage with the doors thrown open became the street before the place of business.

I Edward IV. "Enter two prentices, preparing the Goldsmith's Shop with plate." When Mrs. Shore enters, "The boy departs, and she sits sewing in her shop. Enter the King disguised." Edward's words, as he enters, show that he is walking along the street, looking for this special shop. At the close of the scene she says to Shore, "I prithee, come, sweet love, and sit by me. No King thats under heaven Ile love like thee." The curtain, therefore, closed on the shop scene, and the passage across the outer stage, through the proscenium doors, served as the street.

The Renegado, I, 3. "A shop discovered, Gazet in it. Francisco and Vitelli walking by." During the scene others enter and pass across the stage.

II Honest Whore, III, 3. "Enter at one doore Lodovico and Carolo; at another Bots, and Mistris Horsleach; Candido and his wife appear in the Shop."

In these cases it is plain that the shop is behind the curtain, and, in this last quotation, it is quite evident that the outer stage, with the proscenium doors thrown open, is used as a street. In *Bartholomew Fair* there are at least two shops on the inner stage at one time,—Lanthorn's stall of hobby horses and Ursula's booth where the "best pig" is roasted. Knockem says to Quarlous in II, 1, "This is old Ursula's mansion; how like you her bower?" While the two shops are set, people pass back and forth across the stage as if in a public street.

All the illustrations that have been given so far bear directly on these four parts,—the curtain, outer stage, inner stage, and proscenium doors. Now if we remember the curtain and inner and outer stages in the Messallina picture, the curtain, inner and outer stages, and proscenium doors in the Duke's theater, and add to this the demands of the plays, as shown by the illustrations just given, I think we must conclude that a typical Elizabethan stage had a rear inner stage, a front outer stage, a curtain separating the two, and two proscenium doors.

III. SECONDARY CURTAINS

It is clear that in all the cases quoted in the preceding section the main curtain, hanging under the outer edge of the gallery, is used. (Throughout this study this is always the curtain referred to when the word is used without qualifications.) There are still two other curtains occasionally found on the lower stage,—a second curtain or traverse and a bed curtain. These have not been separated from the permanent curtains by previous writers, and, as a result, the whole question of the hangings has been one of indefiniteness and general misunderstanding. A careful examination of the scene in connection with the whole play will always reveal the particular one used.

A. *Second curtain or traverse*

In certain scenes, a hanging was drawn across some part of the inner stage for the purpose of concealing some person or small object from the characters already using most of the inner stage and the outer. The Restoration inner stage was larger than the Elizabethan, but a situation in the *Duke of Guise*, V, 3, well illustrates the use of this second curtain. After men have been talking on the outer stage for some fifty lines, "The Scene draws, behind it a Traverse."   "The Duke

of Guise is assaulted by Eight." At the end of this scene,
Guise "flings himself upon him [the assassin]. Dies." Just
then "The Traverse is drawn. The king rises from his Chair,
comes forward, etc."

Merchant of Venice, II, 7. "Enter Portia with Morocco
and both their traines." The scene is a room in Portia's
house, where the choice of caskets is to be made. Portia
says to her maid, "Goe, draw aside the curtaines, and discover the severall Caskets to this noble Prince: Now make
your choyse." Here is simply a small part of the inner stage
curtained off to conceal the caskets until the proper moment
to discover them.

Valentinian, II, 4. Everything in the great hall has been
especially prepared to dazzle and charm Lucina. She enters
amid song and music, and by and by, according to prear-
rangement, "Jewels shew'd." Lucina at once says, "Nay,
ye may draw the Curtain, I have seen 'em, but none worth
half my honesty." Here again there is a small space curtained off on the inner stage to reveal the jewels at a certain
moment, so as to create the desired effect on Lucina.

Volpone, V, 1. "*Volp.* Go, straight give out about the
streets, you two, that I am dead. *Exeunt Cast. and Nano.*
Mos. What do you mean, sir? *Volp.* O, I shall have
instantly my Vulture, Crow, Raven, come flying hither, on the
news, to peck for carion, my she-wolf, and all, greedy, and full
of expectation. . . . Get thee a cap, a count-book, pen and
ink, papers afore thee; sit as thou wert taking an inventory
of parcels: I'll get up behind the curtain, on a stool, and
hearken; sometime peep over, see how they do look, with
what degrees their blood doth leave their faces. O, 't will
afford me a rare meal of laughter!" They are all the while
in a room using a table, chairs, etc., so that the curtain is
drawn; but some corner or part of the inner stage is enclosed,
so that the old Fox may be hid from the greedy flatterers,
and yet be visible to the audience.

Duchess of Malfy, IV, 1. The scene is a room in the
Duchess's palace. After the action has continued for some
time, "Here is discover'd, behind a travers, the artificiall

figures of Antonio and his children, appearing as if they were
dead." A small space on the inner stage closed by a traverse
is all that is here implied.

Old Fortunatus, II, 1. The Soldan is royally entertaining
Old Fortunatus at his court. After he has shown the stranger
many different things and come to admire him very much, he
decides to display his greatest treasure: he "draw[s] a curtaine," and reveals a golden box which contains the magic hat.

In all these cases there can be no uncertainty about the
curtain referred to: 1. they are already using part of the
inner stage with the curtains drawn, as is shown by the distinct location of the scene and the use of properties [1]; 2.
the space does not need to be large to contain these objects,
and, more than this, in most cases it must be small in order
to make the scene effective.

B.   Bed curtains

Trick to Catch the Old-One, IV, 5. "Dampit in bed;
Audrey spinning by." After the scene opens Audrey sings
a song appropriate to the occasion; at the end of which, Dampit
calls out, "Trahe, trahito, draw the curtain; give me a sip
of sack more." Here the curtains, which plainly belong
to the bed, remain closed till after the song, when Dampit
awakens, and calls for sack, thus making an effective opening
for the scene.

What You Will, II, 1. "Laverdure drawes the curtaines;
sitting on his bed, apparalling himself; his trunke of apparaile
standing by him."

Witch, IV, 2. "He's asleep, lady, the curtains drawn
about him."

The Rape of Lucrece, IV, 3. Sextus enters Lucrece's room
"with his sword drawn and a taper light." In the midst
of his soliloquy, he says:

> "Heere, heere, behold! beneath these curtains lies
> *Lu.   discovered in her bed.*
> That bright enchantresse that hath daz'd my eyes."

[1] For full information of this point see Chapters V–VI.

I Honest Whore, I, 3.   The time has come for Infelice to awake from her unnatural sleep.   The Duke, Doctor, and two servants enter her room; the Duke gives orders to "lock the doores," and then to "uncurtaine her."   His commands are obeyed, and Infelice is discovered lying on her bed.

II Iron Age, IV, 1.   "Loud musicke.   Enter Egistus with his sword drawne, hideth himselfe in the chamber, behind the Bed-curtaines."

Sophonisba, I, 2.   "The Ladies lay the Princesse in a faire bed, and close the curtaines, whil'st Massinissa enters." After a few lines spoken by the women, "Enter foure Boyes, antiquely attired, with bows and quivers, dauncing to the cornets, a phantastique measure; Massinissa, in his night-gowne, led by Asdruball and Hanno, followed by Bytheas and Jugurth.   The Boyes draw the curtaines, discovering Sophonisba, to whom Massinissa speakes."

II   Antonio and Mellida III, 4.   "*Maria.* Good-night, Nutriche.   Pages, leave the roome. . . *Exeunt Pages and Nutriche.*   O thou cold widdowe bed. . . *Maria draweth the courtaine: and the ghost of Audrugio is displayed, sitting on the bed.*"

This, as well as the other illustrations, shows without explanation the use of the bed curtains as distinct from the others.   There was also, occasionally, a curtain temporarily hung on the outer stage, as in the *Spanish Tragedy*.   This was a mere makeshift for a play within a play—the preparation of the stage being part of the scene—and in no sense one of the regular hangings.   The confusion of the different curtains is due, partially, I think, to the dramatist's loose use of the terms "curtain," "curtaines," "arras," "traverse," etc.   The word which suited the meter, or the sound of the lines, or the situation, or gave variety, or indeed the one which suggested itself first to the writer's mind, seems to have been used.   In the *Looking Glass for London*, II, 1, the King says, "Now ope, ye *foldes*."   "He drawes the *Curtaines* and finds her stroken with Thunder, blacke."   In the following illustrations, there can be little doubt that one and the same curtain is meant, and yet various words are used.

Whore of Babylon, Prologue. "He drawes a *Curtaine* discovering Truth in sad abiliments; uncrowned; her haire disheveld, & sleeping on a Rock. Time (her Father) attired likewise in black, and al his properties (as Sithe, Howre-glass and Wings) of the same Cullor."

Dido, I, 1. "Here the *curtains* draw:—there is discovered Jupiter dandling Ganymede upon his knee, and Mercury lying asleep."

Distresses, IV, 1. "He steps to the *arras* softly, draws it. Claramante is discovered sleeping on her Book, her Glass by."

King of Lombardy, V, 1. "A *canopy* is drawn, the king is discover'd sleeping over Papers."

The White Devil, V, 4. Flamineo says: "I will see them, they are behind the *travers*. Ile discover their superstitious howling." "Cornelia, the Moore, and 3. other Ladies discovered, winding Marcello's coarse."

IV.   SIDE ENTRANCES TO THE INNER STAGE

We have shown that the outer stage contained two proscenium doors, but no mention has been made of the entrances to the inner stage. That there were some kind of side passages to it cannot be doubted. 1. Properties are moved on and off the inner stage. 2. Characters are discovered on the inner stage, and left behind the curtain when the scene closes. 3. Characters playing on the outer stage with the curtain closed often cross behind the scenes from one proscenium door to another.[1]

Any amount of illustrations can not prove, but only suggest, the arrangement of the side passages to the inner stage. Considering the needs of the plays and the principles of acting, it is possible that they took the form of plain "wing entrances." Two or three "wings" to the side, so arranged as to be able to be put in or taken out at pleasure, would make a very practical and simple form of entrance. Such an arrangement solves the difficulty in certain perplexing situa-

---

[1] *Cf. Caesar and Pompey*, IV, 1: and *Fair Maid of the Exchange*, I.

tions in the plays[1]; it lends itself to scenes of overhearing and stealing in and out, as it allows a passage without the noise of creaking doors, and throws the stage open to uncertainty and expectation[2]; it gives an opportunity for mechanical devices[3]; it provides an opening through which characters may look off the stage and describe some object at a distance[4]; it allows a straight and mysterious passage across the stage.[5]

V. GALLERY

A.   A fair-sized gallery closed by a curtain

In the Messallina picture there is a gallery over the inner stage, extending from the curtain hangings to the rear wall, a space 20 to 25 feet wide and 10 to 12 feet deep.   The early plays abound in the use of this structure as the walls of a city, a fort, or a prison.   There is scarcely an extant chronicle play which does not have a parley from this elevation, or men stationed here defending the supposed enclosure.   The presence of the stage gallery, and its utility in war plays are so generally conceded, that proof of the same seems unnecessary.

It was sometimes used in a play within a play for seating the stage audience.

Spanish Tragedy, IV, 3.   The King and his train pass "into the gallerie," from which they witness the play prepared by Hieronimo.

Women Beware Women, V, 1.   "Enter above, Duke, Bianca, Lord Cardinal, Fabrico, other Cardinals and Lords and Ladies in state."   Before the play of real life and death

---

[1] Cf. *The Wise Woman of Hogsdon*, V, 2.
[2] Cf. *Loyal Subject*, III, 3; and *Humorous Lieutenant*, IV, 1.
[3] Cf. *If this be not a good Play, the Devil is in it*, Scene 4.
[4] Cf. *Eastward Ho*, IV, 1.
[5] Cf. *Macbeth*, IV, 1.

Perhaps just here a note should be made on the occasional reference to a third door to the lower stage.   This door is so seldom specifically mentioned that it cannot have been a permanent fixture.   When the word is used I take it to mean simply a third place of entrance, anywhere through the inner stage, without any reference to a regular door.

opens on the outer stage, Hymen, Ganymede and Hebe enter the gallery, "dance a short dance," and then offer their cups to the Duke. This illustration, besides showing a special use of the gallery, also gives some idea of its size.

It was occasionally used as a prison, or a place of temporary confinement.

Great Duke of Florence, V, 1. "Sanazarro above." After a bitter reflection on his past life and imprisonment, the sound of approaching horses is heard. He rushes to a window, saying, "This Back-part of my Prison allows me Liberty to see and know them."

The Picture, IV, 2. A plan has been formed to punish Ubaldo and Ricardo. They have each gone off with a girl, and Sophia is left alone on the lower stage. Suddenly, "A Noise of clapping a Door: Ubaldo above in his Shirt." "*Ubald.* What dost thou mean, Wench? Why dost thou shut the Door upon me? . . . . 'Slight, 'tis a Prison, or a Pig-stye." In the midst of his raving, the other man unwillingly joins him,—"Ricardo, entering with a great noise above, as fallen." Corsica and Hilario "enter below" and laugh at them, while Sophia reads them a lecture. In the end she assigns them a definite work and the three pass out leaving the captives to their fate. "*Ubald.* I am faint, and must lie down. *Ric.* I am hungry, too, and cold. O cursed women! *Ubald.* . . . But let us rest as well as we can to-night, but not o'er-sleep ourselves, lest we fast to-morrow." Besides showing this particular use of the gallery, this illustration suggests the need of a gallery curtain—the men are left in confinement and not relieved till in the next act.

It served as a higher point of observation, or the upper deck of a ship.

I Fair Maid of the West, IV, 4. "Enter Sailer above." He calls to those below, "Arme Gentlemen, a gallant ship of warre makes with her full sailes this way."

Dick of Devonshire, I, 3. According to orders to "get up to the highest Terret," "Enter Buzzano above." Here he looks out to sea and describes an approaching ship.

It occasionally became a bedroom

Alphonsus, King of Germany, I, 1. Alphonsus "opens the door and finds Lorenzo sleep a loft." When he enters, "Lorenzo Riseth, and snatches his sword which hung by his Bed-side." In the end, the Emperor kills him and "exit," but no provision is made for removing the dead body or the bed and other properties. From this it seems that the scene must have been discovered and closed by a curtain.

Massacre at Paris, I, 5. "The Admiral discovered in his bed." In scene 7, Gonzago enters and kills him, and the Guise, apparently on the lower stage, says, "Throw him down." If these two scenes may be taken together, they show that the bedroom was in the gallery and closed by a curtain.

Another illustration of the gallery curtain is found in the *Unnatural Combat*, V, 2. Malefort exclaims, as he enters, "Ha! this is the Fort. Open the Gate. Within there." In reply he is met by "Soldiers with muskets," who refuse him entrance. By and by they "thrust forth Theocrine; her Garments loose, her Hair dishevell'd" to her longing father, but only to die in his arms. "Montrevile above, the Curtain suddenly drawn," laughs out, "Ha, ha, ha!" and continues to jeer until "Soldiers enter above" and call him away. The fact that this is a fort, and that soldiers enter to him, makes it pretty certain that Montrevile is in the gallery; therefore, gallery curtains.

B.   Gallery doors

The stage directions in the plays demand at least two entrances to the gallery: the fact that there were only two possible sides for regular passageways makes it practically necessary to have a door on either side of the gallery.

Rape of Lucrece, V, 3. "Enter in severall places, Sextus and Valerius above."

Directions to the characters in the plays indicate this arrangement.

Cruel Brother, V, 1. Castruchio discloses his plan to the Duke: "Be you within your Bed, to free you from the world's suspicion: whilst I do place behind the Gallery door

(which leads into your Closet Chapel) such bold Fellows, as
shall dare to thrust their weapons home."

C. Gallery window

Messallina shows a small square curtain at the rear of the
gallery which undoubtedly closes a window. There are
frequent situations in the plays in which an opening to the
outside is needed, and, on the whole, the location of the
window in the Messallina seems to be very plausible.

Great Duke of Florence, V, 1. "Sanazarro above" is
pacing his prison when he hears the patter of horses' hoofs
in the distance. He rushes to some opening, saying, "This
Back-part of my Prison allows me Liberty to see and know
them." Here he remarks to himself the different ones he
sees coming.

The Picture, IV, 2. "Ubaldo above" examines the
prison in which he has suddenly found himself: "The Windows grated with Iron, I cannot force 'em, and if I leap down
here, I break my Neck."

I If You Know not Me, V. "Enter Elizabeth, Gage,
and Clarentia above," Elizabeth says, "Good Master Gage,
looke to the pathway that doth come from the Court." He
goes to some window and there describes three horsemen
riding towards them with all speed.

I have already given two cases of looking off to sea from
this location, which would require an opening. The window
closed by a curtain in the Messallina serves all these purposes
very well, and I believe was a regular feature in a typical
Elizabethan stage.

VI.   BALCONY WINDOWS

The situation in *David and Bethsabe*, I, 1, where "He
[the Prologue] draws a curtain and discovers Bethsabe, with
her maid, bathing over a spring; she sings, and David sits
above viewing her," was always a mystery to me until I saw
the cuts of the Duke's theater with its balcony windows just

over the proscenium doors. This seemed a happy suggestion for the Shaksperian stage, and examining the plays with this in mind, I have been fully convinced that such was the arrangement. These windows would of course indicate a room behind them, with a floor on the same plane with the gallery, but in practice little more than the opening itself could be used. Each gallery door regularly becomes an entrance to this supposed room on either side of the gallery.

First may be given a few instances where one character directs the actions of another in a play.

Family of Love, I, 1. Glister says to Maria, "I will sequester you from all rooms in my house save this gallery and your upper chamber." Scene 2. Gerardine, coming to take his leave of her, says to his confidants, "Peace: let's draw near the window and listen if we may hear her." Maria soon appears and among other remarks says, "I prithee, love, attempt not to ascend my chamber-window by a ladder'd rope: th' entrance is too narrow." III, 1. Maria and her lover are talking, presumably in the gallery, when they see Lipsalve enter. Gerardine whispers: "But who comes here? —let's remove ourselves to the window, and observe this piece of man's flesh." They disappear, and presently, "Enter Gerardine and Maria above." These directions become intelligible, if we conceive of Maria being allowed the liberty of the gallery and her private chamber at the side with its balcony window.

Cruel Brother, V, 1. Castruchio says to the Duke: "Be you within your Bed, to free you from the world's suspicion; whilst I do place behind the Gallery door (which leads into your Closet Chappel) such bold Fellows, as shall dare to thrust their weapons home."

Loyal Subject, II, 3. Under pretense of visiting, the Duke has come to search the house of his Loyal Subject. He says to Archas, "Lead on, we'l follow ye: begin with the Gallery, I think that's one." Archas answers, "'T is so, and 't please ye, Sir, the rest above are lodgings all."

Characters frequently speak of various houses built on this plan.

Wit without Money, III, 1. "A back door opens to a long gallerie."

Women beware Women, III, 1. " 'T is a sweet recreation for a gentlewoman to stand in a bay-window and see gallants."

Chaste Maid, V, 1. "We 're simply stock'd with cloth-of-tissue cushions to furnish out bay-windows."

The many courtship scenes from windows are excellently adapted to this arrangement. The word "window" is almost always used, and the broad open gallery would be a poor representation of a window to a room.

Monsieur Thomas, III, 3. "No light in any window," says Launcelot, as the serenade begins. Presently, Mary and her Maid appear "above," and the latter sings:

> ' Come up to my window, love, come, come, come,
>   Come to my window, my dear,
>   The wind, nor the rain shall trouble thee again,
>   But thou shalt be lodged here."

A rope ladder is lowered, and Thomas is "climbing to promotion," when "Madge with a Devil's vizard roaring, offers to kiss him, and he falls down." As he cries out, "O my leg, . . . Oh, a Surgeon, a Surgeon, or I dye," Mary comes out "below," but finding his moans only a trick to get her out, she steps back and locks the door behind her.

The Captain, II, 2. "*Fabrico*. Whence is this musique? *Frederick*. From my Sister's chamber." "Enter at the Window, Frank and Clora." They "warble their woodnotes wild" from this height, but fortunately the Captain falls asleep and does not hear the slighting remarks which they make about him after the song. Fabrico says, "Let 's awaken him, and away." "If he hear this, not all the power of man could keep him from the windows till they were down and all the doors broke open." Shortly after this the women exeunt, saying, "Shut the window."

Chances, IV, 3. "*Pet*. 'T is so; that house, Sir, is it: out of that window certainly I saw my old Mistresses face. *Musick.—Enter Bawd above. Pet*. Look ye there, Sir, do ye know that head? *Fred*. I should know that face."

Blurt Master Constable, IV, 1.   Curvetto finds, as he enters, a "cord hanging from the window." "Stay, here's the door, the window; hah, this, this! Cord?—umph!—dear cord." As he pulls the cord, down comes a pail of foul water on his head, at which he exclaims, "This sconce shall batter down those windows." They answer above: "Why do you beat our doors? . . . . This was a water-work to drown a rat that uses to creep in at this window."

As already stated, the David and Bethsabe scene in which characters " above " see the action on the inner stage, becomes intelligible only by the balcony-window arrangement ; and this situation is not uncommon in Elizabethan plays.

Love's Sacrifice, V, 1.   "Enter above Fiormodo. A curtaine drawne, below are discovered Biancha, in her night attire, leaning on a cushion at a Table, holding Fernando by the hand." Fiormodo's remarks show plainly that she sees the lovers who are behind the line of the curtain. If she were in the gallery, this would be exceedingly awkward if not impossible; but seated at one of the balcony windows, she easily commands a view of the scene below.

Humorous Lieutenant, I, 1.   The usher says to the ladies, "Madams, the best way is the upper lodgings, there you may see at ease." Soon the King enters and a court scene takes place, part of which must be on the inner stage.

Emperor of the East, I, 2.   A court is being held before Theodosius and Pulcheria. The former is struck by the beauty of one in the crowd, and asks his eunuchs to bring him "to some place where" he "may look on her Demeanour." Pulcheria alone continues to hear and dismiss the various suits. Just as she comes to Athenais, "The curtains drawn *above*, Theodosius and his eunuchs [are] discovered."

Michaelmas Term, II, 3.   In come Easy and Shortyard looking for a shop. "*Sho.* Ay; let me see; this is it; sign of Three Knaves; 't is it." The keeper cries: "What lack you, gentlemen? See good kerseys or broadcloths here; I pray come near." Here, while they persuade Easy to sign a heavy bond, "Thomasine above" looks on, making an occasional remark. This transaction must be at the counter, at the edge of the inner stage, but one at a balcony window, could easily see all.

Other illustrations of the window arrangement.

Women beware Women, I, 3. "Bianca and mother appear above." Leantio, who is now leaving, remarks, "See, and she be not got on purpose now into the window to look after me!" They are still lingering here, when the Duke and his procession "pass over the stage in great pomp, and exeunt." Later on in the play, the statements are made: "She spied him from the window." "The Duke himself just spied her at the window." The balcony window as shown in Plate 4 faces the opposite door, so that it offers an advantageous, as well as a secluded, position for observing some one leaving or entering the stage.

Witches of Lancashire, III, 1. "Enter musicians playing before Lawrence, Doughty, Arthur, Shakton, Bantam, Whetstone, and Gregory, with dishes: A Spirit (over the doore) does some action to the dishes as they enter." This train was most likely through the proscenium doors, and the Spirit could find no place to lodge "over the doore" unless there was an opening there.

Henry VIII., V, 2. Dr. Buts, seeing the treatment which Cranmer is receiving, hastens to inform the King. Presently "Enter the king and Buts, at a windowe above." After Henry has seen the situation, he says, "Let 'em alone, and draw the curtain close; we shall hear more anon." [1]

In conclusion, no one doubts that the Elizabethans knew the art of acting. Facial expression is of the greatest importance in this, and only by means of these cross-corner balcony windows can this be secured for the character on the lower stage in communication with another "above." The many passionate love scenes which took place at this part of the stage would lose half their effect if the face of the lover could not be seen. What would that beautiful moonlight scene, at the balcony window, between the world's famous lovers be, if Romeo must stand with his back to the

[1] *The Devil is an Ass*, II, 2, has a unique use of the balcony window in connection with the gallery.

audience? The construction on our own stage for this scene is never at the rear, but always at the side.

VII. THE "HUT"

In the pictures of the theaters on the Bankside, there is seen a small house projecting above the main building, which is usually known as the "hut." The chief purpose of this structure is neither hard to conjecture nor to prove. Far back in the Miracle plays, ascending and descending with suitable machinery was a well-known device. This idea would naturally be carried directly down into the Elizabethan drama and make its demands felt in the building of the regular theaters. The "hut" over the stage is the result.

This elevated structure must provide room not only for the machinery but for carrying out the action as well: in order to make the scene at all effective, the characters and vehicles must be concealed here before the descension and pass up completely out of sight in the ascension. The "hut" of the Hope theater, as shown in the Visscher map, extends from a fourth to a third of the way across the building. Making a general estimate from this and from the function of the little house in the plays, I should say it was a building about twenty feet square, projecting ten feet forward and backward over the gallery curtain, so as to provide a means of ascent from both gallery and outer stage. To the fore-part of the "hut" was attached a shade or "shadow," which served as an additional covering for the outer stage. The base of the "hut," and the ceiling of the gallery and shade were all of a piece, and formed the "heavens." Heywood in his *Apology for Actors*, [1] says of the Campo Martio: "The covering of the stage, which we call the heavens (where upon any occasion the gods descended), was geometrically supported by giant-like atlas." This covering, we may suppose, was painted to represent, or at least to suggest, the sky. Perhaps part of the floor of the "hut" was made of canvas or cloth, and

[1] Thomas Heywood, *An Apology for Actors*, 1612. Ed. Collier, Sh. Soc. Pub. 1841.

so arranged that bodies could ascend or descend through it
without any apparent opening. An idea of its working
may be understood from *Coelum Britannicum*, a masque performed at Court in 1633. "And then rising again with a
gentle motion bears up the Genius of the three Kingdomes,
and being past the Airy Region, *pierceth the Heavens* and is
no more seen."

Before subdividing the subject, a few general illustrations
may be given.

Alphonsus, King of Arragon, Prologue. "After you have
sounded thrise, let Venus be let downe from the top of the
Stage."

The Widow's Tears, III, 2. "Musique: Hymen descends;
and sixe Sylvanes enter beneath, with Torches."

Silver Age, II, 1. "Iuno and Iris descend from the
heavens." Act. III, 1. "Mercury flies from above,"
saying, "Thy clamours (Ceres) have ascent through
heaven."

Brazen Age, V. "Jupiter above strikes him with a thunder-
bolt, his body sinks, and from the heavens descends a hand
in a cloud, that from the place where Hercules was burnt,
brings up a starre, and fixeth it in the firmament."

A.   *Descension and ascension over the outer stage*

More Dissemblers besides Women, I, 3. Duchess, Celia,
and the Cardinal are in the gallery watching for the procession
to pass. Soon the victorious Captain enters, and "a Cupid,
descending," sings over him, and "ascends" again.

Wife for a Month, II, 1. "A Curtain drawn. The King,
Queen, Valerio, Evanthe, Ladies, Attendants, Camillo,
Cleanthes, Sorana, Menallo" are all seated on the inner stage.
"A Mask. Cupid descends, the Graces sitting by him, Cupid
being bound the Graces unbind him, he speaks." After
the masque, "Cupid and the Graces ascend in the
Chariot."

Women beware Women, V, 1. The Duke and his train are
seated in the gallery to see the play or masque. As a part

of the performance, "Livia descends, as Juno," over the altar and is killed by the poison fume.

The Witch, III, 3. The scene is a field where the witches are holding a consultation. Towards the close "A Spirit like a Cat descends," and calls to Hecate, "Either come or else refuse." She obeys:

> "Now I go, now I fly,
>   Malkin my sweet spirit and I.
>   O what a dainty pleasure 't is
>   To ride in the air, etc."

Golden Age, V, 1. "Sound a dumbe shew. Enter the three fatall sisters, with a rocke, a thread, and a paire of sheeres; bringing in a Gloabe, in which they put three lots. Jupiter drawes heaven[1]: at which Iris descends and presents him with his Eagle, Crowne, and Scepter, and his thunder-bolt. Jupiter first ascends upon the Eagle, and after him Ganimed."

B. *Descension and ascension over the gallery*

In the last section of illustrations it is fairly clear that the passage of the heavenly characters was through the floor of the hut, projecting beyond the gallery, as they are either above or in contact with those on the lower stage. Descending into the gallery was probably provided for, but seems to have been used very little—perhaps because the distance was short, and, therefore, the descent would be less realistic and spectacular than over the outer stage.

The Scholar, Epilogue. "First to the gallery, in which the throne, to their amazement, shall descend alone."

It would be more appropriate, and was so used occasionally, for falling bodies and trap-door effects.

The Picture, IV, 2. Ubaldo has been locked in the gallery and is unable to escape. Suddenly, he is joined by his friend, who, it seems, fell through the ceiling,—"Ricardo, entering with a great noise above, as fallen." As the dazed man

---

[1] This word does not refer to any part of the stage; but simply to one of the three lots which Jupiter draws.

collects himself, he says: "Zounds ! have you trapdoors ? . . .
Whither am I fallen ?   into hell !"

VIII.   MINOR PARTS OF THE STAGE

A.   Traps

The outer stage, inner stage, and gallery each contained
one or more traps.   The number and exact location of these
are of no consequence even if it were possible to determine
the matter with certainty.

If this be not a Good Play, V.   "As they go off, from under
the ground in severall places, rise up spirits."

Whore of Babylon, IV.   "A cave suddenly breakes open,
and out of it comes Falshood (attir'd as Truth is) her face
spotted, she stickes up her banner on the top of the Cave; then
with her foot in severall places strikes t! ɔ earth and up riseth"
eight characters.

The inner stage needed traps for pitfalls in wood scenes,
heads rising out of fountains, brazen heads speaking, and the
like.   Traps in the gallery were of course only for occasional
situations; for example, the *Jew of Malta*, V, 4, "Enter
Barabas, with a hammer, above, very busy."   He is fixing
a death trap in the gallery for Calymath, but in the end falls
into it himself: "A charge, the cable cut, a caldron discovered
into which Barabas falls."

B.   Stairs

The stairs connecting the upper and lower stages were
located somewhere in the space off either side of the inner
stage.   They were, of necessity, behind the scenes, as the
gallery or balcony window and lower stage are often used in
situations which require the two to be without visible connection: the enemy are besieging a city and the townsmen
enter on the walls and defy them; or a character is in prison
in the gallery or the rooms on either side, and begs those
on the lower stage to help him escape.   Hieronimo in the
Spanish Tragedy takes special care to secure the keys, after
the King and his train have passed into the gallery, so that

he may carry his bloody masque to completion. Finally, and possibly the most definite proof of all that these stairs were behind the scenes, characters passing from the lower stage to the gallery or balcony window, and vice versa, are usually followed by the stage directions "Exit" and "Enter." There should be a second set of stairs on either side of the gallery leading to the "hut," and a third between the basement and lower stage. In brief, there were perhaps three sets of stairs on either side of the stage: the first from basement to lower stage, the second from lower to upper stage, and the third from upper to "hut"—all behind the scenes, and, for the economy of space, the second and third directly over the first.

C. Tiring-house, etc.

The tiring-house and place for properties do not properly belong to the stage, and may, therefore, be dismissed with a word. There is ample room for both in the spaces on the first floor behind the proscenium doors, and on the second behind the balcony windows.

D. Properties

The properties on the Elizabethan stage were sufficient, but few and plain. Their purpose was, first, to give the appearance of a certain location, and second, to permit the lines to be acted out in a realistic manner. Except for the "heavens," which I have already described, there was no painted scenery. The plays have no perspective; the scene just before us is always the thing. Characters look out an opening and describe other places and objects, but the scene itself ends where it begins. The plays do not lend themselves to distant views, but are focussed on the properties on the stage. When the "art of perspective in scenes" came into use at the Restoration the difference in the plays is noticed at once; the stage is no longer the stage, but a part of some vast space.

The majority of the scenes in the Elizabethan drama, using

properties, may be classed under three heads: 1. Room or hall scenes. 2. Scenes of nature. 3. Shop scenes. For the purpose of listing the properties the first two may be subdivided.

1. *Room or hall scenes.* a. *Bedroom;* a bed, table, chairs or stools, and lights are the properties regularly used or mentioned. b. *Hall;* table, chairs, and stools. c. *Presence chamber;* throne, and occasionally table and chairs. d. *Courtroom;* a bar, table, and chairs. e. *Church or temple;* an altar and, if needed, a tomb. Prison scenes may sometimes be included under "b," but usually no properties are mentioned except fetters and chains.

2. *Scenes of nature.* a. *Woods or park;* large and small artificial trees, mossy banks, and sometimes a rock or two. b. *Garden;* small artificial trees or shrubbery, and benches.

3. *Shop scenes;* a counter and a few wares to indicate the class of trade to which the shop belongs.

The floor in all scenes was covered with rushes, which were suitable for any setting. If a room, rushes being at that date a regular carpet, they were in place; if a nature scene, they harmonized with the green foliage and lost their identity.

The above are not all the set scenes nor are the properties there listed all those that were ever used, but they are the usual scenes and their usual properties. I say again the setting was plain and simple, but amply sufficient to create the proper illusion and to meet all the demands of the lines. Even after the Restoration the setting was often very meagre and plain. *Spanish Friar*, II, 2. "Scene, A Chamber. A table and wine set out." *Limberham*, I, 1. "An open garden house; a table in it and chairs." *Wild Gallant*, IV, 1. "Table set with cards upon it. Trice walking."

Each part of the stage has now been considered separately, and in conclusion I will discuss briefly the drawings, as a summary to the chapter. I have used the following figures and suggestions from the Fortune Contract: the height of the three galleries, 12, 11, and 9 feet respectively,—retaining the first, or 12 feet, as the height of the stage gallery; the depth

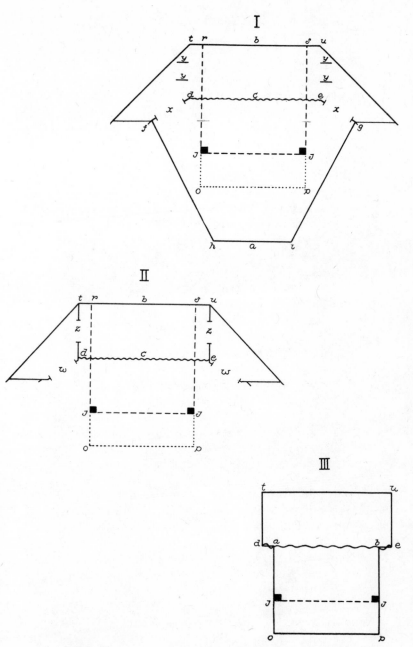

PLATE 8.—A TYPICAL SHAKSPERIAN STAGE—GROUND PLANS

of the second gallery, 13⅓ feet, as the combined depth of the off-set, 3⅓ feet for the cross-corner proscenium doors, and the inner stage, 10 feet; the stage posts "with carved proportions called Satires," railing, and "shadow." The following are from the Messallina picture: the converging outer stage with its railing; the figured curtains; and the suggestion of a brick wall in the rear of the gallery. The only point in the perspective view (Plate 4) that needs explanation is the curtain arrangement. As it is impossible to form a proper idea of the space behind the hangings with the curtains closed, the left curtain to the inner stage is drawn and the right closed, while the right gallery curtain is entirely removed and the left partly drawn. The exact dimensions of all parts of our reconstructed stage according to the plans in Plate 8 are as follows:

I. Plan of the lower stage, showing also the relative position of the "hut" and shade. Broken lines indicate the "hut," dotted lines the shade, and waved lines the curtain. jj are the stage posts, xx the proscenium doors, dce the curtain, $yyyy$ the "wings," $higedf$ the outer stage, $deut$ the inner, $rjjs$ the "hut," and $jopj$ the shade. The distance from h to i is 15 feet, f to g 39 feet, a to c 26⅔ feet, j to j 20 feet, j to o 6 feet, j to r 20 feet, d to e 25 feet, and b to c 10 feet.

II. Plan of the upper stage, showing also the relative position of the projecting "hut" and shade. The line-marking is the same as in I. ww are the balcony windows $deut$ the gallery, dce the gallery curtain, and zz the gallery doors. The distance from d to e is 25 feet, and d to t 10 feet.

III. Plan of the "heavens." This represents one plane formed by the base of the "hut" and the ceiling of the gallery and shade. The broken line indicates the connection of the "hut" and shade, and the waved line the suspended gallery curtain. The dimensions of the "hut" and shade have been given in I, and the gallery in II.

The proscenium doors and balcony windows are from 6 to 7 feet wide; the inner stage is 12 feet high and the gallery 13 feet, making the "heavens" 25 feet above the lower stage.

This reconstruction attempts to be a typical stage of the

Elizabethan period, or rather an effort to show the principal parts of that stage in their relation to each other. The architecture and special shaping of the various parts perhaps differed with each theater: the Fortune stage was in a square building, and the Globe in an octagonal; the Rose had one "hut" and the Globe two; the outer stage may have been square in its earlier history, and converging in its later; the Fortune may have had posts on the stage, and the Red Bull none; the Blackfriars was roofed, and the Globe "open to the weather." All such individual arrangements are, indeed, objects of great interest, but of no vital effect on the plays. The outer stage with its proscenium doors; the inner stage, its curtain, and side entrances; the gallery, its window, curtain, and doors; the balcony windows; and the "heavens" high over all—these are the parts which were reckoned with by Shakspere and his fellow dramatists in their workshops, and which therefore influenced the construction of their plays. In all points, however, I have aimed at a plain, practical, consistent stage,—a stage for the story-like drama of long ago.

CHAPTER IV

SOME PRINCIPLES OF RESTORATION STAGING

INTRODUCTION

THIS chapter is devoted (1) to a brief description of the method of performing a modern melodrama, and (2) to an investigation of certain principles of Restoration staging which seem to be survivals from Elizabethan times. As such a study in the midst of chapters on the Elizabethan stage is plainly a digression, some explanation of the advantage of treating these two subjects at this point in the essay may be given:

1. There is still an occasional play, especially among the cheaper melodramas, with several scenes to the act, and consequently a special kind of stage is temporarily arranged by the aid of the "drop" and "wings" with doors in them to meet the needs of its production. With the exception of painted scenery and a front curtain, this improvised stage is nothing more than a modified form of the old Shaksperian outer-inner stage—the outer before the "drop" and the inner behind it; and as stage and staging go hand in hand, the method of presenting a play on this new-old stage contains certain principles which were in use in the seventeenth century. Therefore, a brief description of the performance of a modern play with eight or ten scenes, aided by pictures of the stage in each scene, will serve as a practical introduction to the last three chapters of this essay. It will define certain terms which will be frequently used throughout the remainder of the dissertation; it will introduce us to several of the most important principles of Elizabethan and Restoration staging, which are later discussed at length; it will show us these

79

principles in working order on our own stage; and, most important of all, it will fit us to understand without frequent and detailed explanations each step in the study of the Dryden and Shaksperian methods of staging.

2. A careful examination of certain principles in Restoration staging will throw considerable light on the more obscure Elizabethan conditions. As I have already shown, the stage of 1660-1700 was very similar in the arrangement of its parts to the Shaksperian, and in all probability certain laws of staging on the earlier survived on the later. These laws are easily shown in the plays after 1660, because the stage directions are sufficiently explicit; but sometimes with considerable difficulty in plays before that date, because the stage directions are often indefinite or not there at all. The special student of the stage sees that this or that situation in a Shaksperian play was played so and so, but a proof of his ideas that can be presented in a few pages is at times very hard to give. At his hand, however, is a Restoration play with the same situation, and here the action is fully explained by the dramatist's own words. Therefore, since both the Shaksperian and the Dryden theaters had outer-inner stages, the explanation of a scene on the later stage affords some assistance in proving the method of producing the same kind of scene on the earlier. It is for this reason that a brief study of the Restoration stage is necessary in an investigation of the Elizabethan. But instead of interweaving the discussion of the staging of the two periods, it seems advisable to show at the outset, in a separate chapter, the existence of certain principles in the later period; and then, with this knowledge in hand, to proceed to a study of Shaksperian staging. This is the method I have adopted. In the present chapter I have attempted not to make a complete study of the Restoration stage but to show the presence there of a few principles and special features which I believe to be survivals from Elizabethan times. In the last two chapters the Shaksperian method of stage presentation is studied. An effort is there made to prove all points from Elizabethan plays, and Restoration conditions are called on only for confirmatory evidence; but all the while

the knowledge of certain methods of staging in the later period serves as a kind of background, and assures us that we are proceeding in the right way.

I. PRESENTATION OF A MODERN MELODRAMA

With the aid of the cuts in Plate 9[1] and the synopsis on the play-bill, I shall give an outline of the presentation of *The Outlaw's Christmas*, which I witnessed in the American Theater, New York City, on August 7, 1907. This play is a fair illustration of its type, and similar ones may be seen at any time by all who care to visit the so-called "Homes of Melodrama." The term "outer scene" is used here and throughout the essay to mean a scene, usually without properties, on the outer stage; and "inner scene," one on both outer and inner stages with the regular setting on the latter. The words "property" and "properties" refer to any part of the setting except the "flat" scenery.

The Outlaw's Christmas, ACT I, SCENE 1. "On the adjoining roofs of a New York apartment house. The fall of the year." Inner scene. The whole stage was used with the setting shown in Plate 9. Though not noticeable in the scene, the properties were kept well back from the front of the stage. Scene 2. "Boudoir in Anna Robinson's flat. Same day." Outer scene. Just as the first scene closed a "drop" fell on about one third of the stage, cutting off all the properties from view and apparently giving us a new scene. The characters entered through the doors in the "wings"—the old proscenium doors—and the opening in the "drop," and the action was resumed at once on this bare outer stage. It was dignified with the name of a lady's boudoir, but it little resembled one. The action was nothing more than a necessary dialogue, but it was supposed to take place in Anna Robinson's house. Scene 3. "Same as Scene 1. Same day." Inner scene. As the "drop" rose, the front of the stage, which had just been a private room, became a part of the roof scene, and all was in

---

[1] These cuts were drawn from my description of the scenes as they were presented on the stage.

readiness to begin the action without a moment's delay.   It
will be noticed, thus far, that when the "drop" was down the
space before it, though without properties, was a stage in
itself; when the "drop" was raised, the division between the
outer and the inner stages being removed, the two became one,
and the properties ranged on the inner gave the setting for
the whole.

ACT. II, SCENE 1.   "Jack Foster's cabin in the Klondike.
Winter."   Inner scene.   The whole stage was used with the
setting shown in Plate 9.   Scene 2.   "Interior of an abandoned
gold mine.   Same night."   Outer scene.   Once more a
"drop" fell on about one third of the stage, cutting off all
properties, and the characters carrying torches rushed across
the scene by way of the proscenium-wing doors as if in
an abandoned mine.   Scene 3.   "Same as Scene 1.   Two
weeks later."   Inner scene.   The "drop" rose and the whole
stage again became the scene in the Klondike.

ACT III, SCENE 1.   "Grand Canyons in Colorado.   Five
months later.   Summer."   Inner scene.   The whole stage was
used with the setting shown in Plate 9.   Scene 2.   "Lonely
mountain trail.   Same day."   Outer scene.   A "drop" fell
at about the usual place, and the former scene was hidden.
The only property here was a block of wood, which was appropriate in the preceding as well as the following scene, and
consequently remained before the line of the "drop" throughout the act.   The audience was favored with "Specialities"
in this scene, which was simply to give time for preparing the
new setting, which was rapidly taking shape behind the
"drop." Scene 3.   "The shores of the Rio Grande River.
Two weeks later."   Inner scene.   The "drop" rose, and the
space of the mountain trail faded into a rather beautiful scene
representing the banks of a river.

ACT IV, SCENE 1.   "Living room in an old fashioned cottage
on the Palisades, New York.   Five months later."   Outer
scene with three pieces of property.   About one half of the
stage was visible before the "drop," and contained a chair
near one "wing" and a stand with a lamp on it near the other.
Scene 2.   "The Palisades.   Same night."   As the "drop"

PLATE 9.—THE SCENES IN *The Outlaw's Christmas* (1907)

rose on a darkened stage, the chair and stand disappeared through the "wings," and the space of the living room became a part of the wintry out-door scene on the Palisades.

From the method employed in staging this play we are able to deduce certain principles,—principles as old as the Elizabethan drama. The properties used and the nature of the setting in general are of no consequence to us, but the laws observed in the manipulation of this outer-inner stage should be carefully noticed: First, the properties were for the most part confined to the rear of the platform, and changed either during an act-division or during the playing of a scene on the outer stage; second, when the "drop" was down, the space before it was a stage in itself; when the "drop" was raised, the outer and inner stages became one with the action over any part of the two, and the properties in the rear gave the setting for the whole; third, by means of the alternation of outer and inner scenes the action was virtually continuous throughout the act; that is, no time was lost between the scenes except for the lowering and raising of the "drop," which was practically nothing. In addition to these principles, it should also be observed, for the aid it will give us in understanding the Restoration drama, (1) that the localities marked in the text gave no idea of the absence or presence of properties on the stage during the scene, and (2) that though two propertied scenes came together in the last act, the arrangement of the settings and scenes was such that no delay was occasioned in the change.

2. SOME PRINCIPLES OF RESTORATION STAGING

With the foregoing principles before us, we will pass at once to a study of a few laws and special features of Restoration staging. Here the outer-inner stage was a permanent arrangement, and the principles that we have already observed were regularly used in the main body of plays. In the accompanying illustration (Plate 10) may be seen the form of the English stage in 1763. Some changes had already taken place since the days of Dryden. Boxes had been placed on the stage, the balcony windows were little used as such but mainly as gallery boxes, and the outer stage had been abbreviated and the inner proportionately enlarged. But with a proper allowance for these changes, we can from the Fitz-Giggo picture form a fair idea of the Restoration stage. Some distance back on the stage is the proscenium arch where the curtain operates; behind the scenic opening is the inner stage; and before it is the outer stage with a proscenium door and a balcony window on either side, and *without any curtain whatever in front of it.*

The outer stage after 1660 is usually called the "apron," as though it were a mere extension of the inner stage. To anticipate our detailed discussion, we may state here that when the curtain was closed, this outer part was a stage in itself with its own entrances and exits and its own scenes; but when the curtain was drawn, it lost its identity and became part of the inner stage. The curtain would of course be the regular division between the two stages, but as painted scenery was now in use, "flats" at the proscenium arch or a short distance back usually took its place.[1] Perspective on the inner stage would naturally call for painted "flats" to back the outer. These would be more expressive than the curtain, and would in no way whatever affect the principles of stage presentation, which we are about to consider. I shall, therefore, use the terms, "curtain," "flats," and "curtain and flats" indiscriminately in speaking of this division on the stage after 1660

Before attempting to note certain principles in Restoration staging, it seems advisable to give an outline of the stage presentation of a complete play. The terms "outer scene" and "inner scene" will be used with the same significance as in *The Outlaw's Christmas.*

The Fate of Capua, ACT I, SCENE I. "The Senate." Inner scene. The senators are in session discussing their future relations towards Hannibal. The outer and inner stages are

---

[1] An illustration of this may be seen in the illustrated quarto of Settle's *Empress of Morocco.* The cut opposite page 9 of the quarto shows a painted "flat" at the proscenium arch.

PLATE 10.—FITZ-GIGGO—STAGE OF COVENT GARDEN THEATER IN 1763

used as one with the setting on the inner[1] and the action on both. Scene 2. "The Outside of the Palace. Enter Pacuvius with Guards. Virginius heading the Rabble." Outer scene. The "flats" are closed and the action takes place on the outer stage without properties. Scene 3. "Virginius's House. Favonia at work with her Women." Inner scene. The "flats" are drawn and both stages are used as one with the setting on the inner and the action on both.

ACT II, SCENE 1. "The Forum. Enter Decius Magius with Perolla, and two or three of his Clients among the Citizens." Inner scene. The space of both stages is usually needed in the Forum scenes, though of course few properties are used. Scene 2. "Virginius's House. Enter Favonia, a Woman following." Outer scene and part inner.[2] The "flats" close on a small part of the inner stage on which perhaps a few properties are located, but the action takes place mainly on the outer stage. Towards the end of the scene Favonia passes out, and Virginius and Junius enter. Virginius says to his friend, "I need not tell you, you command all here. . . . Rest on my arm, and let me lead you in." Scene 3. "The Scene changes to Favonia's Apartment. Favonia leaning on her Hand in a Chair. Virginius leading Junius into the Room." Inner scene. The "flats" are drawn and the two stages become one with the setting on the inner and the action on both. Here are three scenes in succession, and yet they are so arranged that the action is practically

---

[1] By the term "setting on the inner stage," I mean, as will be explained later, that the regular setting was on the inner stage when the curtains were drawn. The movable properties did not necessarily remain there throughout the action, as the scene, a room, for example, being once before the audience, the tables, chairs, etc., could be moved about on the stage at the pleasure of the actors. The term will be used in this sense throughout the remainder of this study.

[2] This phrase is used when it seems the "flats" were not at the proscenium arch but some distance back on the inner stage, so that the scene included the outer stage and a small part of the inner. There were either no properties or very few that could be removed quickly and without notice, or such as would be in place when the "flats" were drawn.

continuous from the beginning to the end. During the change
from Scene 2 to Scene 3 the characters remain on the stage,
and are now in one room and now in another according as the
"flats" are closed or drawn. Notice the effect secured by this
rapid change; Junius knows the fate which awaits him if he
once again sees Favonia, and would avoid a meeting if possible,
but suddenly and irresistibly he finds himself in her presence.

ACT III, SCENE 1. "A Garden. Enter Pacuvius and Perolla."
Inner scene. The whole stage is used with properties on
the inner to represent a garden. Scene 2. "Virginius's
House. Enter Junius." Outer scene and part inner. The
"flats" are closed, revealing perhaps a small part of the
inner stage. The scene is simply a monologue by Junius, and
no properties are needed. Scene 3. "The Forum. Enter
three or four Citizens of the better sort." Inner scene. Same
as the previous Forum scene. Scene 4. "Scene changes to
Virginius's House. Enter Junius." Outer scene and part
inner. Same as Scene 2. The scene is little more than a
passage across the stage by Junius as he goes to take his last
leave of Favonia. Scene 5. "Scene changes, and shows
Favonia asleep on a Couch in an Undress. Junius returns."
Inner scene. The "flats" of the previous scene draw, and both
stages become the apartment of Favonia. Here the change
from Scene 4 to Scene 5 does not occur with Junius on the
stage as in II, 2–3, because the situation is different. Instead
of a sudden surprise, we need a quiet, reflective opening,—
simply a warning of what is coming, and then a moment to
gaze on that sleeping woman, beautiful and innocent, before
the action is carried into effect.

ACT. IV, SCENE 1. "The Forum. Junius, with Citizens."
Inner scene. Same as previous Forum scenes. Scene 2.
"Scene changes to Pacuvius's House. Enter Pacuvius and
Servant." Outer scene. The scene is short and conversa-
tional, and no properties are needed. Scene 3. "Scene
changes to the Forum. A Crowd of Citizens." Inner scene.
This is the usual Forum scene. Scene 4. "Virginius's
House. Enter Virginius with a Servant." Outer scene and
part inner. Same as III, 4. Virginius says to the servant,

"You know the rest, tell her that I am here." "Ex. Servant." Scene 5. "Scene opens, and shows Favonia on the Ground." Inner scene. Towards the close "A Servant enters with a Dagger in one Hand, and a Bowl in t'other, and gives 'em to Virginius, who places 'em on a Table by Favonia." Soon after this, "The Scene shuts upon Favonia; he goes off." Here again one scene merges into another with characters on the stage during the change. But this time the character on the inner stage comes, by drawing the "flats," into the presence of those on the outer, instead of the opposite, as in II, 5–6.

Act V, Scene 1. "The Forum. Enter Pacuvius, Vibius Virius, and Marius Blosius, with the Senators in their several Parties." Inner scene. Same as previous Forum scenes. Scene 2. "Virginius's House. Favonia enters with a Dagger in one Hand, and a Bowl in t'other." Outer scene and part inner. Same as IV, 4. After a soliloquy, "She drinks, throws the Bowl one way, and the Dagger another." It is evident that no properties are on the stage, as Favonia enters carrying all that is needed.[1] Scene 3. "Pacuvius's House. Pacuvius, Vibius Virius, Marius Blosius, with seven or eight Senators rising from a Feast." Inner scene. The whole stage is used with the properties on the inner and the action on both.

For the sake of referring to this play later, I have stated a number of points which remain to be proved. It is sufficient here to notice that there are marked peculiarities in the staging. There are from three to five scenes to an act; some need properties, others do not, and there is a marked regularity in the alternation of the two classes; scenes change with characters on the stage, etc. These questions will now be taken up separately with a view to establishing the following principles of Restoration staging.

---

[1] In this scene three characters are left dead on the stage. Undoubtedly the curtains closed on them, and as they escaped, the "flats" representing Virginius's house drew, and the curtains parted for the final scene. Since there were no properties to remove, the whole would take only enough time to close and open the curtains.

I. LOCATION OF A REGULAR SETTING

The properties of a regular setting were located on the inner stage, and changed for a new scene either during an act-division or during the playing of a scene on the outer stage.[1] First, we have seen the operation of this principle in the presentation of *The Outlaw's Christmas*. The regular settings there were always on the inner stage, and in Act III, the Grand Canyon scene was changed to the Rio Grande, while the mountain trail scene was being played before the "drop." Second, three of the pictures of the Duke's theater, published in Settle's *Empress of Morocco* in 1673, show a full setting in each case on the inner stage, and not a single property on the outer. Third, numerous situation, such as the following, in Restoration as well as eighteenth-century plays show the presence and necessity of this principle:

Author's Farce, Act III, Scene 1. "The Play-House. Enter Luckless as Master of the Show, and Manager." (Outer scene.) After a few words between these two with regard to the show (Scene 2), "the Curtain draws, and discovers Punch in a Great Chair." (Inner scene.) Scene 3. When the second scene is over and the curtains are closed, Luckless announces the next play. (Outer scene.) Scene 4. "The Curtain drawn up to soft Music discovers the Goddess of Nonsense on a Throne, the Orator in a Tub," etc. (Inner scene.) There were perhaps a few chairs on the outer stage throughout the play, but the regular settings were plainly behind the line of the curtain; and, more than this, Scene 2 changed to Scene 4 while the action continued between Luckless and the Manager on the outer stage.

Historical Register, Act I, Scene 1. "The Play-House. Enter several Players." (Outer scene.) Medley, the author, is describing the first scene to Mr. Sowrwit when the prompter announces that "they are ready." Medley replies, "Then

---

[1] The outer stage in the Restoration, as I have already explained, sometimes included part of the inner; that is, it consisted of the space before the curtains or "flats," the latter of which were occasionally some distance back on the inner stage.

draw the Scene, and discover them." Scene 2. "Scene draws, and discovers Five Politicians sitting at a Table." (Inner scene.) Act II. has a similar opening in which—Scene 1—Medley gives orders to "draw the Scene and discover the Ladies in Council." (Outer scene.) Scene 2. "The scene draws, and discovers four Ladies." (Inner Scene.) Scene 3. The scene ended and the curtains or "flats" closed, a little scene ensues, as usual, on the outer stage. (Outer scene.) Presently the prompter again appears to announce that everything is prepared for the next scene. Medley says, "Then draw up the Curtain," etc. Scene 4. "An Auction-Room, A Pulpit and Forms plac'd and several People walking about, some seated near the Pulpit." (Inner scene.) Here, as in the *Author's Farce*, it is clear that the regular settings were on the inner stage, and in case of Scenes 2, 3, 4, the play continued before the curtain while the stage was being reset behind it.

Rehearsal, ACT V, SCENE I. "Bayes and the two Gentlemen." (Outer scene.) The location of the scene is not marked, and it is plainly on the outer stage. After a very pompous speech by Bayes to the other gentlemen on the great scene he is going to present (Scene 2), "The Curtain is drawn up, and the two usurping Kings appear in State, with the four Cardinals," etc. (Inner scene.)

Soldier's Fortune, ACT IV. During the act the "Scene changes to Covent-Garden Piazza. Enter Silvia and her Maid in the Balcony" Presently Courtine appears below and attempts to climb up to them. As he is swinging in mid-air, "Enter Fourbin and Bloody-Bones, as from Sir Davy Dunce's House," shouting "Murder, Murder, Murder!" Courtine scrambles up into the balcony, and the men hasten on at the sound of Sir Davy's approach. Dunce knocks at his door and enters, after which the "Scene opens in the middle of the House, and discovers Sir Jolly Jumble and the Lady putting Captain Beaugard in order, as if he were dead."

Love Triumphant, ACT V, SCENE I. "Lopez's House." (Outer scene.) At the close of this comparatively brief scene (Scene 2), "A Royal Chamber is discover'd, by drawing the former Scene." (Inner scene.) In this, as well as in the preceding illustration, it seems very probable that the first scenes were mainly outer scenes with "flats" at or near the proscenium arch, which later drew and revealed the set scenes.

In the following instances the elaborateness of the second scenes in a play of eleven scenes shows that over-much time would be consumed if they were left unprepared until the first scenes closed, and also that they occupy too large a space to divide the inner stage with the first scenes. All things considered, there can be little question but that the first scenes were entirely on the outer stage with "flats" at the proscenium arch, and the second ones on the whole stage with the settings on the inner.

Virgin Prophetess, ACT I, SCENE I. "The Grecian Camp." The scene is conversational, and no properties are needed (Outer scene.) Scene 2. "The Curtain draws, and discovers the Town of Troy, with a Magnificent Chariot twenty Foot high, drawn by two White Elephants, placed in the Depth of the Prospect, between two Triumphal Columns; the one bearing the Statue of Pallas, and the other that of Diana, and fronting the Audience. In the Chariot are seated Paris and Helen. In the two front Entryes on each side of the Stage, advanced before the side Wings, are four more White Elephants, bearing, each a Castle on their Backs, with a Rich Canopy over each Castle, and in each three Women; on the Necks of all the Elephants a Negro Guide." (Inner scene.) ACT V, Scene I. "Enter Cassandra." The locality of the scene is not marked, and no properties are needed in the action. (Outer scene.) Scene 2. "The Town of Troy being four Ranges of Buildings, extending to the utmost of the House. Making three several Streets, with each a several back Scene terminating the three Prospects. These Streets are seen through three Gates, Archt nineteen Foot high, with Perculices, Battlements, and Urns. The other Buildings twenty-six-Foot high, some with Rails, Banisters, and Statues, others with Turrets, &c." (Inner scene.)

After all no one has ever seriously doubted that in the Restoration the regular settings were on the inner stage, and were discovered by drawing the curtains or "flats." The stage directions are too explicit and the general conditions of the staging of this period too well known for the fact to be questioned. The method used in changing the settings, however, seems to be largely forgotten, and for this reason it has been necessary to illustrate it by the previous quotations. Further proof of this practice will be found in almost all the illustrations given in support of the other principles.

II.   OUTER AND INNER STAGES BECOME ONE

When the "flats" were closed, the space before them was a distinct stage in itself; when the "flats" were drawn, the outer and inner stages became one and the action took place over any part of the two. This principle, likewise, is already familiar to us from the presentation of *The Outlaw's Christmas*, and its successful use there shows clearly that it is an actual working law on an outer-inner stage and not a theoretical one.

In the picture in Plate 10 may be plainly seen two stages, an outer and an inner. The simple presence of this outer stage with its own entrances and exits is almost sufficient proof in itself that it was a complete stage when the curtains or "flats" at the proscenium arch were closed. That it had its own scenes is evident from the situations in the *Rehearsal*, Act V, Scenes 1, 2; *Author's Farce*, Act, III, Scenes 1, 2, 3, 4; *Historical Register*, Act I, Scenes 1, 2 and Act II, Scenes 1, 2, 3, 4; and many similar ones to be given later.

The union of the outer and inner stages when the "flats" at the proscenium arch were drawn may be shown by situations in which the proscenium doors or balcony windows were used in connection with the set or inner stage:

The Maiden Queen, V, "The Court." Inner scene. The Queen and other ladies are present. In course of the action, "Enter at one Door Lysimantes, at the other Philocles, Celadon, Candiope," etc. If these were, as they seem most likely to have been, the proscenium doors, the entrances to the outer stage became entrances to the inner, and therefore the two stages must have been considered as one,—in this case a royal chamber in the court.

Friendship in Fashion, IV, 1. "Night-Garden. Enter Goodvile at one Door; Mrs. Goodvile, and Lettice following her at the other." Again the proscenium doors were used as entrances to the inner stage, which shows that the whole platform constituted the scene.

Love in a Nunnery, II, 3. "A Night-piece of a Garden." Here the lovers are enjoying a quiet stolen hour, when approaching footsteps are heard. The women exeunt, and presently appear in one of the balcony windows. When Mario and his servants rush into the garden, Laura and Violetta call to him from the balcony for help; and as he is about their rescue, Aurelian and Camillo make good their escape. The balcony windows were just over the proscenium doors and consequently on the outer stage; therefore, their use in connection with a set scene would indicate that no line of division was drawn between the two stages in such a situation.

Soldier's Fortune, ACT IV, SCENE 1. "The Scene opens in the middle of the House, and discovers Sir Jolly Jumble and the Lady putting Captain Beaugard in order, as if he were dead." Sir Davy is sent off to pray for the life of Beaugard, while his wife uses other means to restore him. Somehow the old cuckold fears his prayers are not very effective, and by and by comes to the balcony window to inquire if there are yet any signs of life in the man; his wife assures him there are good hopes, and Sir Davy returns to his devotions.

Sir Martin Mar-All, ACT V, SCENE 1. The scene is a large open court on which most of the action in the play takes place. As one incident in the scene, Sir Martin is to prove to the ladies that he has musical ability. Millisent and Rose take their places in one of the balcony windows, and "Sir Martin appears at the adverse Window." It has been previously arranged for Warner to play and sing behind the balcony curtain, while Mar-All with lute in hand gives the proper appearance of doing the work himself. "A Tune [is] play'd; when it is done, Warner rings, and Sir Martin holds"; but at the end of the second song, "Sir Martin continues fumbling and gazing on his Mistress," and the women across the way fall a-laughing at him. Just at this point John rushes into the court for protection from his pursuers, and Sir Martin, always sure to do the wrong thing at the right time, thinking to regain his lost favor with the ladies, promptly descends and beats off the officers. It is clear here that the whole stage including the proscenium doors and balcony windows made up the scene.

As this discussion shows, the proscenium doors were used as entrances to the whole stage as well as to the outer part. When the curtains were drawn, they served as a means of access to the room, church, or whatever place the scene represented; when the curtains or "flats" were shut, perhaps one of the doors closed represented an entrance to a house, and the other open a street way. Satirical remarks, such as the following, on these time-honored fixtures, when their day was all but over, show the part they played in the action. "Whatever be the performance, and whoever be the personages, they all either walk in and out at the permanent doors which form part of the proscenium, or they slide in and out between the intervals of the wings."[1] "That ligneous barricade which . . . now serves as the entrance of the lowly cottage, and now as the exit of a lady's bedchamber."[1] "The two stage doors . . . that served for palace, cottage, street, or hall, used for each place, and out of place in all."[1]

In conclusion: It has already been noticed that the regular settings were always placed on the inner stage. With this arrangement it would simply be impossible for the outer stage to be otherwise than a part of the inner when the "flats" were drawn. Moreover, a number of situations will be pointed out in the following section in which characters were left on the stage when the "flats" closed, which would show that the characters were previously acting before the proscenium arch. All things considered—the size and arrangement of the two stages, the situations in the plays, and the observance of this principle in practice in *The Outlaw's Christmas*—, there can be

---

[1] Quoted from W. J. Lawrence, *A Forgotten Stage Conventionality*, *Anglia*, vol. xxvi., pp. 259-60.

little question about the use of the outer stage for certain scenes, and the outer and inner combined for others.

III.　THE CONTINUOUS ACT

A Restoration play frequently contains from ten to twenty scenes. If in the performance of such a drama ten or twelve minutes were lost between each scene in rearranging the setting, the life of the play would be killed and the length of the performance would be extended beyond all endurance. To avoid this difficulty the scenes in each act were so written and so staged that one could follow another almost immediately; that is, so that the action in an act could be virtually continuous from the beginning to the end. There were various ways of securing this continuity of action through whatever number of scenes the act might contain, but the only one which need concern us here—in a study of surviving Elizabethan conditions—is the alternation of outer and inner scenes. [1]

[1] Most of the other ways of securing the continuous act in the Restoration grew out of the use of painted scenery,—a feature destined to revolutionize the whole system of staging. A few ways may be mentioned. A change of outer scenes was marked by a change of "flats" at the proscenium arch. Similarly a change of likepropertied inner scenes was occasionally affected by nothing more than a change of back "flats." Perhaps the most interesting and complicated way of avoiding delays between the scenes was the use of varying portions of the inner stage with the outer. This was done by the opening and the closing of "flats" at different distances from the rear of the inner stage. For example, in a succession of room scenes the first occupied the whole stage, the second the outer and a small part of the inner, the third the outer and still more of the inner, the fourth the outer and a small part of the inner, the fifth the outer and all the inner, and so on. Any number of combinations could be used, and each one would give the appearance of a new scene without any loss of time in setting and resetting the stage. Some rearrangement of the setting behind the "flats" usually look place while the scene was playing before them. This was a kind of alternation. It was applicable, however, only where the scenes were all of one class, as room scenes or forest scenes.

Alternation of scenes

A very common method for keeping the action continuous throughout an act was the alternation of inner and outer scenes. This is perhaps the most noticeable feature of Restoration staging. The dozen or more scenes in a play usually fall into two classes,—one requiring properties and the other not; and the inner or propertied and the outer or unpropertied frequently occur in an alternating series. These two kinds of scenes we have already observed in *The Outlaw's Christmas;* and the reason for such a division was very obvious in the performance of that play. While an unpropertied scene was being played before the "drop," a propertied scene was being set behind it; and in this way the locality changed, but the action was not delayed for a moment. The outer scene was no less important than the inner, but it was so written that it could be played before the "drop" without properties. And so were certain scenes written and played in the Restoration.

In the outline already given of the scenes in *The Fate of Capua* the alternation of outer and inner scenes may be seen throughout an entire play. A summary of the scenes in this drama would be as follows: Act I. Inner—outer—inner. Act. II. Inner—outer and part inner—inner. Act III. Inner —outer—inner—outer and part inner—inner. Act IV. Inner —outer and part inner—inner—outer and part inner—inner— outer. Act V. Inner—outer and part inner—inner. In this way—and this way only—the nineteen scenes run through smoothly and rapidly in the "two hours traffic of the stage."

As the proving of this principle by outlining full plays is very cumbersome, and brings in too many questions outside of the point at issue, we must confine ourselves to single acts.

Mithridates, Act, I Scene 1. "The Outer part of the Temple of the Sun." No properties mentioned or needed in the action—outer scene. Scene 2. "The Scene draws, discovering the Inner Part of the Temple," etc. Properties used in the action—inner scene. In this act it is evident that the first scene was played on the outer stage; and at its close, the "flats" drew, revealing the setting on the inner stage, and the action resumed at once over any part of the platform.

Venice Preserved, ACT IV, SCENE 1. "Enter Jaffeir and Belvidera." Locality unmarked—no properties mentioned or needed—outer scene. The two are on their way to the Senate where Jaffeir is to confess the plot. Scene 2. "The Senate-House. Where appear sitting, the Duke of Venice, Priuli, Antonio, and Eight other Senators." Properties used— inner scene. The first scene is purely conversational and the outer stage is sufficient, but the second scene requires a setting and both stages are needed. By drawing the "flats" at the opening of the senate scene, the dreaded assembly is at once before us and no interest in the action is lost through a long delay.

Don Carlos, ACT V, SCENE 1. "Enter King solus." Locality unmarked—no properties mentioned or needed—outer scene. Scene 2. "The Scene draws and discovers the Queen alone in Mourning on her Couch, with a Lamp by her." Properties used—inner scene. At the close of Scene 1, the "flats" drew and the whole stage became the Queen's apartment.

Wild Gallant, ACT I, SCENE 1. Burr's room. Properties used—inner scene. Scene 2. A street. No properties mentioned or needed—outer scene. Scene 3. "Trice is discovered playing at Tables by himself," etc. Properties used—inner scene.

Loyal Brother, ACT IV, SCENE 1. "Enter Ismael, Sunamire, and Arbanes." Locality unmarked—no properties mentioned or needed—outer scene. Scene 2. "Semanthe, melancholy in her Apartment." Properties used—inner scene.

Cambyses, ACT V, SCENE 1. "The Scene drawn, Cambyses is discovered seated in a Chair sleeping," etc. Properties used—inner scene. Scene 2. "The Palace." No properties mentioned or needed in the action—outer scene. Scene 3. "The Scene open'd appears a Temple of the Sun," etc. Properties used— inner scene. During the playing of the second scene the setting for the first was removed and another placed for the last.

Fatal Marriage, Act. I, Scene 1. "The Street." No properties mentioned or needed in the action—outer scene. Scene 2. "Fernando's House." Properties used—inner scene. Scene 3. "The Street." No properties mentioned or needed in the action—outer scene. Act V, Scene 1. "Enter Biron, Nurse following her." No properties mentioned in the text or needed in the action—outer scene. Scene 2. "Scene drawn, shews Biron asleep on a Couch." Properties used—inner scene. Scene 3. "Scene changes to a street." No properties mentioned in the text or needed in the action—outer scene. Scene 4. "Scene changes to the inside of the house." A chair needed in the action—outer scene and part inner. Scene 5. "Scene opened, shews Pedro on a rack." Properties used—inner scene.

She Would if She Could, Act III, Scene 1. "The New-Exchange. Mistress Trincket sitting in a Shop. People passing by as in the Exchange." Properties used—inner scene. Scene 2. "Sir Oliver's Dining-Room. Enter Sir Joslin and Servant severally." No properties mentioned in the text or needed in the action. This heading is similar to that in *The Outlaw's Christmas*, I, 2. Scene 3. "The Bear." Properties used—inner scene. During the second scene on the outer stage, the shop setting was cleared away and chairs, tables, etc., brought on for the lobby in the inn.

Love and Revenge, Act IV, Scene 1. "Enter Nigrello." Locality unmarked—no properties mentioned in the text or needed in the action—outer scene. Scene 2. "A Room of State." Properties used—inner scene. Scene 3. "A Grotto. Enter Lewis, Brisac, Souldiers with a Page carrying a dark Lanthorn." No properties mentioned in the text or needed in the action—outer scene. Scene 4. "The Scene open'd; Claramount and Fredigond are discover'd together." Properties used—inner scene.

Empress of Morocco, Act IV, Scene 1. "Enter King, Attended." No properties are mentioned in the text or needed in the action—outer scene. Scene 2. "The Scene open'd, is presented a Prospect of a Clouded Sky, with a Rainbow. After a Shower of Hail, Enter from within the Scenes,

Muly Hamet and Abelcador." Properties used—inner scene.

The list of illustrations showing the alternation of outer and inner scenes could be extended indefinitely, but these few must suffice. In truth, any one familiar with the Restoration drama will realize that an effort to prove the alternation of outer and inner scenes in the plays of this period by a handful of quotations is like attempting to establish the Law of Gravitation by a few examples. It is an ever-present and all-important principle. Without the alternation of propertied and unpropertied scenes the proper staging of Restoration plays would simply be impossible.

SPECIAL FEATURES OF RESTORATION STAGING

Closely connected with these three principles of Restoration staging are several special features obtaining in the writing and stage presentation of plays of this period, which should be noticed for the light they throw on similar conditions in the Elizabethan drama.

A. Scenes change with characters on the stage

There are many instances in the plays from 1660 to 1700 where the scene changes from one locality to another with characters on the stage. Perhaps the scene is being acted on the outer stage as in a street or some unlocated place; at the proper moment the curtains or " flats " draw, revealing a certain setting which gives the whole stage the appearance of a new scene, and the characters in action, magic like, find themselves in a different locality.

An Evening's Love, Act IV, Scene 1. The scene is unlocated but presumably a street, as Maskal waits here to give Don Melchor orders as he passes to meet Aurelia in the Garden. After several incidents have taken place and all the characters but Wildblood have passed off the stage (Scene 2), " The Scene opens and discovers Aurelia and Camilla; behind them a Table and Lights set on it. The Scene is a Garden with an Arbour in it. The Garden door opens." Wildblood, after a short soliloquy, passes out, and Melchor enters. A hysterical scene in the garden follows, at the close of which Aurelia "runs out shrieking," and Camilla, who has been hid under the table, "rises up, overthrows the Table and Lights, and runs out. The Scene shuts." Scene 3. The Don is left alone before the "flats." Other characters enter to him and the scene is again a public place as before. The first scene needs no properties, and the action is on the outer stage before the "flats." It represents a street or some public walk, and the characters meet, greet each other, and pass freely in and out the proscenium doors. Suddenly the "flats" draw, and the whole platform becomes a garden by the illusion of the properties on the inner stage. In time the "Scene shuts," and the action continues on the outer stage as in some general passage way. Characters are on the stage all the while. In the first change Wildblood finds himself suddenly transported from a public place to a garden; and in the second change, Melchor passes without taking a step from a garden to a street.

Tyrannic Love, ACT V, SCENE 1. The characters enter "at one Door" and "at the other," and no mention is made of the locality. Maximus, being unable to persuade St. Katherine to his wishes, orders them to "draw then that Curtain, and let Death appear." Scene 2. "The Scene opens, and shews the Wheel." Felicia and her daughter are about to be bound to this instrument of death when "Amariel descends swiftly with a flaming Sword, and strikes at the Wheel, which breaks in pieces; then he ascends again." Shortly after this "The Scene shuts," and (Scene 3) Maximus and Placidus are left on the outer stage. Valerius enters to them with the news that "the Princess and her Mother are no more." The King is so enraged that he kills the messenger, and "spurns the body." Scene 4. "Here the Scene opens, and discovers Bernice on a Scaffold, the Guards by her, and amongst them Porphyrius and Albinus, like Moors, as all the Guards are"; and the play concludes with this setting. In this act there are four scenes—outer, inner, outer, inner—all following each other without a moment's loss of time. Characters are on the stage all the time; now nowhere in particular, and now in a room of torture; again without location, and finally in a place of execution.

Duke of Guise, ACT V, SCENE 1. "The Castle of Bloise." Shortly after the scene opens, "Enter Deputies of the Three States: Cardinal of Guise, and Archbishop of Lyons, at the Head of 'em." No conclusion can be reached for the Succession, and "Exeunt Omnes, but the King." Here the "flats" must have closed, leaving the one remaining character alone on the outer stage. Scene 2. Grillon enters to the King, reveals his plot to kill the Duke of Guise, and the two "exeunt severally." Scene 3. "The Scene opens, and discovers Men and Women at a Banquet, Malicorne standing by." Song and dialogue follow, after which the "Scene closes upon the Company," and Malicorne is left alone before the "flats." Scene 4. Melanax enters to him and claims his soul, and the scene ends in their sinking together. Scene 5. A room in the Court. Scene 6. "Before the Council-Hall." Scene 7. "The Scene draws, behind it a Traverse. The Guise is assaulted by Eight." Scene 8. "The Traverse is drawn. The King rises from his Chair, comes forward with his Cabinet Council." During this one act—and the play has five—eight successive scenes are presented. As I have indicated throughout the illustration, the propertied and unpropertied scenes alternate with each other,—inner, outer, inner, outer, inner, outer, outer and part inner, inner. In the change from Scene 3 to 4 and 7 to 8, characters are on the stage, and are supposed to change their location though they do not necessarily change their position on the stage.

B. *"Flats" used as doors*

Another feature of Restoration staging, which is very strange in itself and perhaps entirely forgotten to-day, is the use of the "flats" as doors to a house or room.

Evening's Love, V, 1. The scene is a garden with a house in the rear. Don Alonzo has lost his nieces, and enters the garden in a rage with "six Servants, with Lights, and Swords drawn." He insists on searching the house, and Bellany, being unable to dissuade him, finally orders his servant to "open the Door." "Maskal goes to one side of the Scene, which draws and discovers Theo[dosia], Jac[intha], Aur[elia], Beat[rix], Cam[illa], Lop[ez], Wild[blood], standing all without motion in a rank." After the old Uncle has satisfied himself of all within, Bellany says, "Now come away, Sir. . . . Maskal, shut the Door." "Maskal goes to the Scene, and it closes."

Soldier's Fortune, V, 1. Sir Davy Dunce shouts to his men, "Break down that Door, I 'll have that Door broke open, break down that Door, I say." . . . "Scene draws and discovers Beaugard and Lady Dunce."

Fatal Marriage, V, 5. "*Fred*. What cries are those? *Vil*. Open that Door." "Scene open'd, shews Pedro on a Rack."

Duke of Guise, III, 1. The scene is an open court by the palace. The populace pass on and only Grillon is left on the scene. In the midst of a soliloquy, he remarks, "the Presence opens"; the scene from this on is a room in the palace with the King and other members of the court present.

Love for Love, IV, 5. "Valentine's Lodging." In response to an inquiry for Scandal, Jeremy says, "Mr. Scandal is with him, Sir; I 'll knock at the Door." "Goes to the Scene which opens." Scene 6. "Sir Sampson, Valentine, Scandal, Jeremy, and Lawyer. (Valentine upon a Couch disorderly dress'd.)"

We have now passed in review three principles and two special features of Restoration staging, and, in conclusion, we may summarize them. Principles: 1. The properties of a regular setting were located on the inner stage, and changed for a new scene either during an act-division or during the playing of a scene on the outer stage. 2. When the "flats" were closed, the space before them was a distinct stage in itself; when the "flats" were drawn, the outer and inner stages became one and the action took place over any part of the two. 3. The action in an act, regardless of the number of scenes, was virtually continuous from the beginning to the end. One method of securing this continuity of action was the alternation of outer and inner scenes. Special features: 1. The scenes were occasionally changed with characters on the stage. 2. The "flats" were sometimes used as doors.

CHAPTER V

THE SHAKSPERIAN METHOD OF STAGE PRESENTATION

AFTER a brief study of Restoration staging, we find ourselves on familiar ground on turning to the Elizabethan.   In Chapter III it was pointed out that with the exception of the gallery the stage of Dryden contained the same number and arrangement of parts as that of Shakspere.   The stage after 1660 recieved some important additions, such as the "art of perspective in scenes," which tended to change the relative importance and size of the two parts of the platform; but it was still an outer-inner stage.   In Chapter IV certain laws obtaining in the writing and performance of Restoration plays were shown,—laws especially adapted to the double form of stage.   These principles certainly did not come from France with its picture-frame stage, and they were too firmly established at the outset to have had no earlier history.   Does it not seem probable that they were simply a continuation, in a slightly modified form, of laws already established on the Elizabethan outer-inner stage?

Indeed we have substantial and well-developed germs of this system in the old religious drama.   In the miracles and moralities there were a number of propertied and unpropertied scenes given on and between the scaffolds, and the action passed rapidly from one scene to another.   The interludes, being confined to one platform without a curtain to conceal the change of properties, limited themselves to one setting for each production. Comparing this custom with Restoration conditions, we find the old division of scenes, propertied and unpropertied, and the action continuous, at least throughout the act; and also a stage which might be called a folded

form of the stage upon which *Mary Magdalene* was performed,
so arranged as to accommodate the two classes of scenes without delaying the action.   Is it not, therefore, reasonable to suppose that the old system was early adapted to the permanent
stage, and continued without serious change throughout the
seventeenth century?

All these, however, are but strong antecedent probabilities,
and the principles of Shaksperian staging remain to be established by evidences in the Elizabethan drama.   We shall begin
this study, as we did that of the Restoration, by giving an
outline of the scenes in a complete play.   Since the principles
are concerned mainly with the parts of the lower stage,—
outer and inner stages, curtain and proscenium doors, we
need only substitute the word "curtain" for "flats" and the
previous nomenclature will suffice.

Merchant of Venice, Act I, Scene 1.   A *street*.   Outer scene.
The meeting of the Venetians; Bassanio reveals his secret need
to Antonio.   The action before the closed curtains without
properties.   Scene 2.   A *room* in Portia's house.   Inner
scene.   Portia and Nerissa talking over the various suitors.
The curtains drawn and the action on both stages with room
properties on the inner.   Scene 3.   A *street*.   Outer scene
The Jew and Bassanio meet and a loan is effected.   The
action before the closed curtains without properties.

Act II, Scene 1.   A *room* in Portia's house.   Inner scene.
Morocco's first meeting with Portia.   The curtains drawn and
the action on both stages with room properties on the inner.
Scene 2.   A *street*.   Outer scene.   Launcelot meets his father,
old Gobo.   The action before the closed curtains without
properties.   Scene 3.   A *room* in Shylock's house.   Inner
scene.   The Clown taking his leave of Jessica.   The curtains
drawn and the action on both stages with room properties
on the inner.   Scene 4.   A *street*.   Outer scene.   Launcelot
meets Lorenzo and delivers Jessica's letter.   The action before
the closed curtains without properties.   Scene 5.   *Before
Shylock's house*.   Outer scene.   Shylock leaving for the
banquet.   The action before the closed curtains without
properties; one door closed as an entrance to Shylock's house.

Scene 6. *Same as Scene* 5 except that the balcony window over the closed door is used. Outer scene. Jessica throws down the bags of gold to Lorenzo and later steals away with him. Scene 7. A *room* in Portia's house. Inner scene. Morocco makes his choice of caskets. The curtains drawn and the action on both stages with room properties on the inner. Scene 8. A *street*. Outer scene. Salanio and Salerino talking of Shylock and Antonio. The action before the closed curtains without properties. Scene 9. A *room* in Portia's house. Inner scene. Arragon makes his choice of caskets. The curtains drawn and the action on both stages with a room setting on the inner.

Act III, Scene 1. A *street*. Outer scene. Shylock raging over his lost daughter and ducats. The action before the closed curtains without properties. Scene 2. A *room* in Portia's house. Inner scene. Bassanio chooses the right casket. The curtains drawn and the action on both stages with a room setting on the inner. Scene 3. A *street*. Inner scene. Antonio following Shylock with a last plea for mercy. The action before the closed curtains without properties. Scene 4. A *room* in Portia's house. Inner scene. Portia and Nerissa take their leave for Venice. The curtains drawn and the action on both stages with a room setting on the inner.

Act IV, Scene 1. *A court of justice.* Inner scene. The trial of Shylock. The curtains drawn and the action on both stages with court-room properties on the inner and extended onto the outer. Scene 2. A *street*. Outer scene. Gratiano overtakes Portia and Nerissa and delivers the rings. The action before closed curtains without properties.

Act V, Scene 1. Portia's *garden*. Inner scene. The home-coming. The curtains drawn and the action over both stages with a garden setting on the inner.

Without regard to all the stage business that I have indicated in the outline, it is noticed that there are nineteen scenes in the play; that some would naturally require properties, as the room and garden scenes, and others not, as street scenes; that one act is not given up to one class of scenes and another to another, but that there is an alternation between the propertied and the unpropertied. In short, there is here a more or less perfect system, based on certain fundamental principles of Elizabethan staging, which we are now to study in detail. Each principle will be taken up separately, and illustration given from the plays to prove the same.

I. LOCATION AND CHANGE OF A REGULAR SETTING

The properties of a regular setting were located on the inner stage and changed for a new scene either during an act-division or during the playing of a scene on the outer stage.

City Madam, ACT I. Scene 2 is a street, as is shown by the frequent remarks: "Do not shew a foolish Valour in the Streets —But in the Day, and View of all that pass by—I' th' Street too." (Outer scene.) But before the close, occurs the stage direction, "A Table, Count-Book, Standish, Chairs, and Stools set out." The next scene is a counting room in Rich's house; "Enter Sir John, Hoyst, Fortune, Penury, Goldwire." (Inner scene.) Sir John's first words, as he faces his debtors, are, "What would you have me do? reach me a Chair." Here in the midst of a street scene is a direction to set the stage with a table, stand, chairs, stools, etc.,—just such properties as are used in the next scene, a counting room. We cannot believe that a manager would disturb an important scene by setting the stage for a coming one. There is, however, but one alternative, namely, that the properties were being arranged for the room scene on the inner stage behind the closed curtains while the street scene was being played on the outer. By this means the curtains could draw at the close of the first scene, and the second could take place at once. If this supposition is correct, the stage direction, carelessly retained in the printed copy, was intended only for the stage hands, and would, therefore, need to be in the previous scene. That it was such a direction is supported by a later situation in the play. In the first part of Act III there is the stage direction, "Musick come down." Seventy-three lines after that, "Enter Goldwire like a Justice of Peace, Ding'em like a Constable, the Musicians like Watchmen." It is evident here that the first direction was intended only for members of the company, and, as such, is perfectly correct in its location in the text. The musicians came down at this point and made ready for their entrance later as watchmen. So it seems that the stage direction in the first instance is genuine of its kind, and that the setting for the counting room was being prepared on the inner stage with the curtains closed while the street scene was in progress on the outer.

Bussy d'Ambois, ACT I. Scene 1 represents an unlocated place, where Monsieur first meets Bussy, and persuades him to go to the court. (Outer scene.) In the midst of the scene in the text is the stage direction, "Table, Chesbord, & Tapers behind the Aarras." There is no need of any furniture in this scene, but the second one uses these very properties. It represents a room in the court, and the King, Queen, and ladies are present. (Inner scene.) Here they are enjoying themselves, some talking, others playing chess, when Bussy is ushered in by Monsieur. Again we seem to have a direction to the stage hands to prepare the room scene "behind the Arras" while the conversational scene is going on before it.

The Cruel Brother, ACT III, SCENE 2. "Enter Lucio and Foreste." (Outer scene.) The scene is unlocated; perhaps it represents a street. Two men meet, and after a short conversation pass on. Before the close of the scene in the text there occurs the direction, "Chair at the Arras." No chair is mentioned in the lines or in any way needed in this scene but the following one uses this property. Scene 2. "Enter Luinna and Duarte." (Inner scene.) The women are in a room: "*Luin.* I would not be unmanerly, but if she be at leisure, tell her I am here. *Duart.* Please your Ladiship to sit, I 'll tell her so."

The Cruel Brother, ACT V, SCENE 1. "A Chair at the Arras. Enter Foreste solus." (Outer scene.) Foreste makes a short soliloquy of nineteen lines, ending with the words, "The darkness of the Night is troublesome. Stay—That sickly light from her Chamber comes. Minion I 'll begin with you." He is supposed to be somewhere without Corsa's chamber. Scene 2. At his exit, "Enter Corsa and a Boy." (Inner

scene.) Presently Foreste enters, and the boy is sent out of
the room. A passionate dialogue ensues, at the end of which
Foreste commands Corsa, "Come, stretch down your arm, and
permit this Scarf to fasten it to the Chair." He cuts her
"wrist veins," "she bleeds her soul away," and he passes
out leaving her dead in her chair. Scene 3 is conversational
without any apparent location or need of properties (Outer
scene), and is followed by a room scene in Foreste's house.
Scene 4. "Enter Foreste, and Servants with Light." (Inner
scene.) He has just dismissed the servants when shouts are
heard without: "Break ope the Door, break ope the Door,
break ope the Door." . . . "Enter Lucio and Servants."
Lucio is in great excitement: "O my Wife! . . . Just
now I lighted from my Horse, enter'd her Chamber: and found
her newly murder'd in her Chair. My Servants say that my
arrival there did just succeed your departure from her."
Foreste answers, "Dismiss your Servants, and you shall know
all." To finish the act: Scene 6 is a street or some public place
(Outer scene); Scene 7 is a bed-chamber with the King lying
abed (Inner scene); and Scene 8 is at a door to a room (Outer
scene). While no curtains are mentioned in the text, they
must have opened and closed with each propertied scene. In
Scene 2 there is no other way provided for Corsa to get off the
stage, and, more than this, the words of Lucio, that he found
her in "her Chamber" "newly murdered in her Chair," show
that she was left sitting where she died. Therefore, the purpose of the first stage direction seems to be this: as Scene 1 was
very short and needed no properties, the inner stage was set
during the act-division. At the close of the monologue,
which was on the outer stage with a faint gleam of light shining
through the hangings, the curtains drew, and the properties
were already arranged on the rear stage for the room scene in
Corsa's house.

The Rape of Lucrece, ACT V, SCENE 3. A battle is raging
and Horatio (at one of the proscenium doors) is valiantly
defending the supposed bridge. (Outer scene.) At the same
time apparently, the stage hands are busily setting the stage
for a new scene; for in the midst of Scene 3 in the text is the

stage direction, "A Table and Lights in the Tent." The next scene represents a tent with Porsenna in communication with his secretary. (Inner scene.) This direction can hardly be explained otherwise than as the preparation of the tent scene behind the closed curtains. In this way the clash of arms on the outer stage would in no wise be interrupted, and the fourth scene could follow as soon as the noise of battle died away.

The Guardian, Act III, SCENE 7. The scene is before Severino's house. (Outer scene.) Scene 8. A room in Severino's house. (Inner scene.) "Enter Jolante (with a rich Banquet and Tapers) in a Chair, behind a Curtain."

Satiro-mastix, ACT I, SCENE 1. A marriage procession crosses the stage on its way to church. (Outer scene.) Scene 2. "Horrace sitting in a study behinde a Curtaine, a candle by him burning, bookes lying confusedly; to himself." (Inner scene.) In this and the previous illustration there is no explanation about the time of preparing the second scenes, but it is explicitly stated that the properties are behind the line of the curtain. As the settings are prepared when the scenes open, and the first scenes require nothing more than a bare space for the action, it seems very probable that the properties were arranged for the inner scenes while the outer were playing. Notice the effect secured by the quick succession of the scenes: in the *Guardian*, Severino returns to his home after a long absence, hoping to bring joy to a faithful wife, but scarcely has he entered, when the curtains draw and present a scene very different from that the weary home-comer had expected; in *Satiro-mastix*, as the procession passes, Crispinus and Demetrius are instructed to wait upon Horace with the request that he write an epithalamium. Just as the last exit is made, the curtains draw, and reveal the poet in his study puzzling his brain over a worthless poem.

In addition to the foregoing proofs of this principle, all the discovered scenes might be cited as showing one phase of the same; namely, the location of the properties of a regular setting on the inner stage. A few illustrations may be given to explain my meaning:

Downfall of Robert Earl of Huntington, III. 2. "Curtain opens: Robin Hood sleeps on a green bank, and Marian strewing flowers on him."

Whore of Babylon, Prologue. "He [the Prologue] drawes a Curtaine, discovering Truth in sad abiliments; uncrowned: her haire disheveld, & sleeping on a Rock: Time (her father) attired likewise in black, and al his properties (as Sithe, Howre-glasse and Wings) of the same Cullor, using all means to waken Truth, but not being able to doe it, he sits by her and mourns."

Brazen Age, II, 2. "Two fiery Buls are discovered, the Fleece hanging over them, and the Dragon sleeping beneath them."

Insatiate Countess, I, 1. "The Countesse of Swevia discovered sitting at a table covered with blacke, on which stands two black tapers lighted, she in mourning."

David and Bethsabe, I. 1, "He [the Prologue] drawes a curtaine and discovers Bethsabe, with her Maid, bathing over a spring."

A Wife for a Month, III, 1. "Enter divers Monks, Alphonso going to the Tomb, Rugio and Frier Marco, discover the Tomb and a Chair."

After all, why should we expect to find a heterogeneous, chaotic setting on the outer stage, and the properties changed before the audience? Hundreds of years before the existence of *Hamlet* and *King Lear*, when the drama was still in the church, the different scenes had their own *sedes* and *plateae*. In the miracles and moralities of later days the same form of staging was observed; and in the interludes, the action being confined to one space, the same setting was generally used throughout the play. Why then should staging have so degenerated during our greatest dramatic period? Some incongruities of course existed, and a list of rather glaring examples could easily be collected, but these are the exceptions and not the rule. Any small unnoticeable object could remain on the outer stage throughout the play; special settings were frequently placed there, and occasionally a very plain normal setting was arranged before the curtain: but the placing and replacing of a regular setting in full view of the audience never was a *general custom*.   It is contrary to the very nature of the stage,—an illusive, make-believe world.

II.   OUTER AND INNER STAGES BECOME ONE

When the curtains were closed, the space before them was a stage in itself; when the curtains were drawn, the outer and inner stages became one, and the properties on the inner stage gave the setting for the whole.   The size, shape, and location of the outer stage—a large space, projecting well into the audience with its own entrances and exits—would seem almost sufficient proof in themselves of the first part of this principle. On turning to the plays, illustration of its use, such as the following, in which characters are already in action on the outer stage when the curtains draw, are comparatively numerous:

Lust's Dominion, ACT I, SCENE 1.   "Music sounding within: Enter Queen Mother of Spain with two pages: Eleazar, sitting on a Chair: the Curtain is suddenly drawn."   During the scene between the Queen and Eleazar some one knocks at the door.   "Eleazar shuts them in," and (Scene 2) "Alvero enters."   A scene follows here between the two, evidently on the outer stage; after which (Scene 3) "The curtains being drawn, there appears in his bed King Philip, with his Lords."   The stage directions here show quite clearly that Scene 2 was before the closed curtains, and also that the time of its playing was occupied with the resetting of the inner stage.

White Devil, ACT V, SCENES 4–5.   "Enter Flam and Gasp at one dore, another way, Giovanni, attended."   After several incidents have taken place, Florence enters with the news that Cornelia has grown wild with grief over her dead boy. Flamineo says: "I will see them.   They are behind the travers.   Ile discover their superstitious howling."   "Cornelia, the Moore and 3. other ladies discovered, winding Marcello's coarse."

Henry VIII, ACT II, SCENES 2–3.   "Enter Lord Chamberlaine, reading his letter."   Presently "Enter to the Lord

Chamberlaine, The Dukes of Norfolke and Suffolke." After a brief discussion of the influence of Wolsey on the King, "Exit Lord Chamberlaine, and the King drawes the Curtaine and sits reading pensively."

Using the principle already established, namely, that the properties of a regular setting were located on the inner stage, the second part of this principle may be proved by illustrations in which the proscenium doors or balcony windows were used in combination with the inner stage. The first two fixtures were on the outer stage, and if characters entered a set scene through the proscenium doors, or took part in the action of a set scene while in the balcony windows, the whole platform must have been regarded as one stage when the curtains were drawn.

An almost unlimited number of illustrations, such as the following, in which the proscenium doors were used as entrances to a set stage, could be given:

I If You Know not Me, III, 1. Elizabeth and her maid are sitting asleep in a room in the home of Beningfield. "Enter Winchester, Constable, Barwick, and Fryers: At the other door, two Angels."

Bondsman, V, 3. The scene represents a court of justice, and the judges are seated in their places. "Enter at one Door Leosthenes and Timagoras; at the other, Officers with Pisander and Timandra."

Love and Honor, V. 2. The scene is a council chamber with the Duke in state and the court around him. "Enter Evan. Mel. Guards at one door, Alv. Prof. Leo. at the other door."

City Madam, V, 3. During the banquet scene, Sir John orders the spirit of Orpheus to appear and to render again "those ravishing strains with which he moved Charon and Cerberus to give him way to fetch from Hell his lost Eurydice." "Musick. At one Door Cerberus; at the other, Charon, Orpheus, Chorus."

The following will serve to illustrate the use of the balcony windows in connection with a set scene:

Love's Sacrifice, V, 1. "Enter above Fiormodo. A Curtaine drawne, below are discovered Biancha, in her night attire, leaning on a cushion at a Table, holding Fernando by the hand."

Emperor of the East, I, 2.   During a court scene on the lower stage, "The curtains drawn above, Theodosius and his eunuchs discovered."

David and Bethsabe, I, 1.   "He [the Prologue] draws a curtain and discovers Bethsabe, with her maid, bathing over a spring; she sings, and David sits above viewing her."

In Chapter III it was shown that the characters "above" in these situations were at one of the balcony windows.   Their connection, therefore, with set scenes while being stationed on the outer stage, shows conclusively that the scenes occupied both stages.

This principle, as we have already seen, formed an important factor in the system of staging during 1660–1700.   If it was indispensable on a later outer-inner stage, it must also have been essential on an earlier.   It must be granted that the law is a very plausible one and grows directly out of the arrangement of the stage and the location of the properties.   Just as was stated in connection with this principle in Restoration play-production, the setting being on the inner stage and the outer lying between it and the audience, the two stages must necessarily become one when the curtains are drawn; the eye irresistibly glides over the level floor and sees only the properties in the background.

III.   THE CONTINUOUS ACT[1]

By means of the alternation of outer and inner scenes,

[1] A thorough study of the division of an Elizabethan play into acts is greatly needed.   Such an investigation may show that some of the details in this section, such as the number and position of the act-divisions, need to be changed; but I believe it will not affect the general principle which I am here trying to explain.   Some light has been thrown on this question in two short studies: Brander Matthews, *Why Five Acts;* and W. J. Lawrence, *Music in the Elizabethan Theater*, in *Shakespeare Jahrbuch*, 1908.   A doctor's dissertation on the subject by Mr. B. W. Stair is to appear soon in Columbia University Studies in English.

8

and the succession of outer as well as certain inner scenes, the action in an act, regardless of the number of scenes, was practically continuous from the beginning to the end.   Before taking up this principle under the two headings, succession and alternation, it may be useful to notice the nature of Elizabethan scenes.   With regard to the setting, they are of just three kinds: first, those in which properties are used, as room scenes, forest scenes, etc.; second, those in which no properties are needed in the action or mentioned in the lines, as street scenes, battle scenes, wall scenes, and the like; third, those in which no properties are needed, and which could be played either with or without a setting, as the many conversational scenes.   The first kind are regularly inner scenes, the second outer, and the third are divided between the two according to the needs of each situation.   An examination of an Elizabethan play shows the arrangement of outer and inner scenes in an order far too regular to be a mere coincidence.   In truth, every one must feel that there lies hidden in this system a principle which the dramatists, consciously or unconsciously, always obeyed in writing their plays.

A.   Succession of scenes

1.   OUTER SCENES.   As outer scenes were played before the curtain without properties and without a painted "flat" at the rear to distinguish one street or public place from another, two or three such scenes could occur in succession without confusing the action.   With one proscenium door closed, that side of the stage could as well represent the front of Brabantio's house as Shylock's; with the doors thrown open, the outer stage would be sufficient for a street, a battle-field, or any open place.   So far as the ground is concerned, all places are much the same, and without properties or scenery, this bit of space would take its location from the lines and the characters. A street scene could be followed by a parley from the walls of a city by drawing the upper curtains and revealing the gallery with certain characters upon it; or it could be followed

by a courtship scene with a Juliet in one of the balcony
windows and a Romeo on the lower stage. With the doors
closed, two or more conversational scenes, apparently in
a house, could likewise occur in succession before the curtains if no properties were needed in the action.   Here, I
believe, many of the shipboard scenes were acted without
a single property. The characters usually do nothing but
rush in with a great hurrah, give or receive a few orders,
and exeunt in the same frantic manner; so that the ship
could belong to either party, according as the "blue" or
the "gray" was on the scene. There seems no need of illustrating this part of the principle from the plays. We have
shown in a previous section that the outer stage was the regular place for the unpropertied scenes, and a glance at any
modern edition of Elizabethan plays, in which the editor has
marked the locality of the scenes, will show a succession of
street scenes, battle scenes, etc., which usually require no
properties.[1]

2.   INNER SCENES.   If two or more inner scenes contained
practically the same settings, they could occur in succession
without changing the properties.   It has already been stated
that the customary properties for a room were a table, chairs,
and stools.   With such a plain and general setting, the stage
might represent a room in Mr. A's house as well as in Mr. B's,

[1] This is perhaps a misleading reference, as the place indications
prefixed to every scene in modern editions of Elizabethan plays are,
of course the interpolations of the editors, and often represent the
wildest kind of guesses.   The headings, "A Street," or "A Field," are
however, often trustworthy, for the scenes are not usually marked
in this way unless the lines plainly call for a street or a field, and there
is no opportunity for a more specific localization.   The most difficult
task before the editor of to-day, and the one which he usually performs
badly, is the localization of what I have called on page 114 the third
class of scenes.   This class is made up largely of conversational scenes.
Very often two or more characters meet for a necessary dialogue; but
the place of their meeting is in no way indicated, and doubtless neither
author nor audience thought of its having any particular location.
Such scenes, which it is plainly evident the author had no thought of
localizing, should be headed "A Place," or "A Scene on the Outer
Stage."

if there was no special attention called to the properties. A throne was the main piece of furniture in a presence chamber, and, therefore, there is no reason why Porrex's court should differ from Ferrex's. Wood-settings were likewise very simple so that scenes supposedly in different parts of the forest could follow each other without change. Illustrations from the plays of the succession of inner scenes are not necessary. A room in X's house is followed by a room in Y's house, or a scene in one part of a forest is succeeded by one in another, and there is an end of it. It should be stated, however, before leaving this part of the principle, that although the succession of outer scenes and the succession of similar inner scenes are of common occurrence, a long series of either is seldom found. Such a series would lead to monotony, and the very existence of the outer-inner stage came from a demand for a rapid and frequent change of scene.

B. Alternation of scenes

Another means of keeping the action in progress during the act was the alternation of inner and outer—propertied and unpropertied—scenes. One scene took place on the outer stage without properties, and another on the two stages combined with the regular setting on the inner; and in both cases the action was mainly before the line of the curtain. In the discussion of this method, I shall first give an outline of the scenes in an entire play, then show the presence and necessity of alternation in a number of single acts, and end by showing the operation of both parts of the principle of the continuous act in a typical Elizabethan play.

Blurt Master Constable, ACT I, SCENE 1. A *room*. Properties used—inner scene. A banquet scene. Scene 2. A *street* before Blurt's house. No properties needed or mentioned—outer scene. "Here dwells the constable." Act II, Scene 1. A *street*. No properties needed or mentioned—outer scene. Men meet on their return from playing tennis. Scene 2. A *room*. Properties used—inner scene. A banquet scene. Act III, Scene 1. A *street*. No properties

PLATE II.—TIMON OF ATHENS, V, 3. INNER SCENE.

Enter a Souldier in the Woods, seeking Timon.
" *Sol.*—Timon is dead, who hath out-stretcht his
            span,
        Some Beast reade this; There do's not
            live a Man.
        Dead sure, and this his Grave, what's on
            this Tomb."

needed or mentioned—outer scene. Music before a window. Scene 2. *Before a monastery.* No properties needed or mentioned—outer scene. Violetta meets Fontinelle. Scene 3. A *room.* Properties used—inner scene. Ladies are sitting at a table. Act IV, Scene 1. A *street.* No properties needed or mentioned—outer scene. A balcony window scene. Scene 2. A *room.* Properties appropriate—inner scene. "Enter Lazarillo bareheaded, in his shirt, a pair of pantables on," etc. Scene 3. A *street.* No properties needed except a rope-ladder—outer scene. A balcony window scene. Act V, Scene 1. A *place.* No properties needed or mentioned—outer scene. Conversational. Scene 2. A *room.* Properties used—inner scene. "O, lie still, lie still!" Scene 3. A *street.* No properties needed or mentioned—outer scene. "Stand, stand; here's the house." The localities of the scenes in this play, thirteen in number, are of course not marked in the quarto, but it is evident that some are indoor scenes and some outdoor, the former requiring properties and the latter not. Between these two classes of scenes—the one played on the outer stage and the other on both—there is an almost regular alternation, which would allow the action to continue without interruption through each act.

Monsieur Thomas, ACT V, SCENE 1. A street. No properties needed or mentioned—outer scene. Hylas waiting for Dorothy "as she comes back." Scene 2. A bed-chamber. Properties used—inner scene. "A Bed discovered with a Black-moore in it." Scene 3. A street. No properties needed or mentioned—outer scene. Hylas meets the supposed Dorothy as she is returning. Scene 4. A room in a nunnery. Properties appropriate—inner scene. "Musick singing." The Abbess with Cellide and the nuns. Scene 5. A place. No properties needed or mentioned—outer scene. The scene consists of only seven lines, and is entirely unlocated; Michael is inquiring for Valentine. Scene 6. A street. No properties needed or mentioned—outer scene. Hylas meets Sam, and tells him of his recent marriage. Scene 7. A room in a nunnery. Properties appropriate—

inner scene. "This gentle Ladies Lodge." Monsieur, dressed as a woman, is caught by the Abbess. Scene 8. A street. No properties needed or mentioned—outer scene. Hylas meets Dorothy on her way home from the nunnery. Scene 9. A hall. Properties needed—inner scene. All the regular characters, one after another, are ushered into a hall in Valentine's house.

Pilgrim, ACT V, SCENES 1-2. A wood. Properties used—inner scenes. The second follows the first without change. In both scenes the woods are several times referred to: "We'll cross these woods—here in the Thicket—in these woods." Scene 3. A place. No properties needed or mentioned—outer scene. The Governor talking with Verdugo and some citizens somewhere in the town. Scene 4. A wood. Properties used—inner scene. Roderigo and Pedro are sitting "in the woods," where "the wind blows through the leaves," and the "birds sing softly." Scene 5. Before a mad-house. No properties needed or mentioned—outer scene. Seberto and Curio have come to inquire after Alphonso, a prisoner in the asylum; at the end Seberto says, "Let's in, and visit him." Scene 6. Within a church. Properties used—inner scene. "Holy Altar, daign to take these for our selves."

Royal King and Loyal Subject, ACT III, SCENE 1. A place. No properties needed or mentioned—outer scene. This is a short scene, and entirely unlocated; the Clown, Mary, and Audley meet and talk. Scene 2. A royal chamber. Properties used—inner scene. "Sound: Enter the King, Clinton, Bonville, Prince, Princesse." Isabella is ushered in by Chester, and becomes the "Soveraignes Bride." Scene 3. Before a house. No properties needed or mentioned—outer scene. The Captain and the Clown come to the door,—"here will we knock." Scene 4. A room. Properties used—inner scene. The Captain and Clown are now in a room, and the mistress of the house bids the Clown, "sit upon my knee my sweet boy." Scene 5. A room. Properties used—inner scene. The king says, "Lords, and the rest forbeare us till we call, a chaire first, and another for our Queene."

Maid's Tragedy, Act V, Scene 1.   A bed-chamber. Properties used—inner scene. The "King abed" is killed by Evadne. Among others who enter at the servants' shouts of "Treason, Treason!" is Lisippus, the new King. He is weeping over the dead body of his brother, when Strato rushes in with the news that "Melantius has got the Fort," and is rapidly collecting men. The King says, "Follow all; for this must have a sudden stop." Scene 2. "Enter Melant. Diph. and Cal. on the wall." The scene is before the walls of the fort. No stationary properties needed or mentioned— outer scene. The King and his men enter presently, a parley is held, and Melantius submits to terms of peace. Scene 3. A room. Properties needed—inner scene. As Amintor comes, Aspatia says, "Please it your Lordship to command your man out of the room."

Wife for a Month, Act II, Scene 1. A place. No properties needed or mentioned—outer scene. Scene 2. A room. Properties used—inner scene. Scene 3. A room. Same as Scene 2. Scene 4. Before the court. No properties needed or mentioned—outer scene. Scene 5. A dressing room. Properties needed—inner scene. Valerio, with his friends around him, is being dressed for the masque. Scene 6. A hall. No properties needed or mentioned—outer scene. The clown and others are holding the doors against the citizens, who are besieging them for entrance to the masque; finally they hear the music and know the King is coming. Scene 7. A large room. Properties used—inner scene. "A Curtain drawn. The King, Queen, Valerio, Evanthe, Ladies, Attendants, Camillio, Cleanthes, Sorano, Menallo. A Mask. Cupid descends, the Graces sitting by him, Cupid being bound the Graces unbind him, he speaks." In the last part of this act we have a dressing-room scene, then a mock scene on the outer stage, and last, the curtains being drawn, a masque scene in which the whole stage is used. Scene 6, humorous of course, has no vital connection with the main action, but while the Clown was cracking his jokes at the door, the properties of the dressing-room scene were being removed and a new setting placed for the audience in the masque; so that when all was ready, the curtains could draw and the play begin at once. The masque, being the important part of the scene and calling for ascending and descending, was most likely on the outer stage, and the mock audience on the inner. The gayly dressed court, seated in the rear, and not speaking till after the play was all over, formed a perfect background for the light, graceful, mythological masque.

The Captain, ACT V, SCENE 1. A place. No properties needed or mentioned—outer scene. (Curtains closed—doors open.) The Father, as if by chance, meets Lodowick and Piso; after they are gone, Angelo and Julio pass this way. Scene 2. A room. Properties used—inner scene. (Curtains drawn— doors closed.) Clora, Frank, and Frederick are all trying to devise some way to get the Captain into the house. He has come as far as the door but will not enter. They first try the experiment of throwing foul water on him from a window (reported action) with the hopes that he will rush in for revenge, but still he does not appear. Last Fabritio decides to go out and insult him, and possibly in a rage Jacomo will follow him in. Scene 3. A street before the house. No properties needed or mentioned—outer scene. (Curtains closed—doors open.) As the Captain is walking along sniffing and complaining at the water thrown on him, Fabritio appears, strikes him, and runs off with Jacomo following. Scene 4. A room. Properties used—inner scene. (Curtains drawn—doors closed.) As the scene opens, Clora shouts, "Be ready for I see Fabritio running, and Jacomo behind him." Just then Fabritio bursts in and the enraged Captain after him. "Fred., Clor., and Maid, lay hold on Jacomo. They drag him to a chair and hold him down in 't." By the inner stage being set with room properties, these outer and inner— street and room—scenes can follow in rapid succession by simply opening and closing the curtains. And here not only a change, but a swift one, is necessary. Jacomo is round about the house all the while, and if Scene 4 cannot follow Scene 3 almost immediately, the whole effect of the trick is lost.

The Mad Lover, ACT V, SCENE 1. In the temple. Proper-

PLATE 12.—TIMON OF ATHENS, v, 4. OUTER SCENE.

Trumpets sound. Enter Alcibiades with his
Powers before Athens.
" *Alc.* Sound to this Coward, and lascivious
Towne, Our terrible approach."
Sounds a parly. The Senators appeare upon
the Wals.

ties used—inner scene. (Curtains drawn—doors closed.) The Princess having begun her devotions, the Nun "draws the Curtain close." Scene 2. A place. No properties needed or mentioned—outer scene. (Curtains closed—doors open.) The scene is conversational and unlocated, but distinctly not in the church. Scene 3. In the temple. Properties used — inner scene. (Curtains drawn — doors closed.) "Enter Nun, she opens the Curtain to Calis. Calis at the Oracle." Scene 4. A street. No properties needed or mentioned—outer scene. (Curtains closed—doors open.) A number of characters pass; some are on their way home from the temple. Scene 5. Council chamber. Properties used—inner scene. Curtains drawn—doors closed.) The King is in council with his sister, when Polydor is borne in. As already noted, the second and fourth scenes need no properties, and have no connection whatever with the temple or the council chamber; while the first, third, and fifth are clearly located, and each requires a special setting. The opening and closing of the curtains, which is plainly stated in two cases, with the accompanying alternation of outer and inner scenes solve the difficulty. By this means all these brief incidents can be given in rapid succession, and yet each have its proper setting.

Wit without Money, Act V, Scene 1. A room. Properties needed—inner scene. (Curtains drawn—doors closed.) The Widow sends word to her sister that she will remain "at home this evening," but later orders her coach made ready quickly. Scene 2. A street. No properties needed or mentioned— outer scene. (Curtains closed—doors open.) Four different crowds pass over the stage, a few of each being overtaken by the next. Scene 3. A bed room. Properties used—inner scene. (Doors closed—curtains drawn.) Valentine says, as one knocks at the door, "Fling up the bed and let her in." Scene 4. A street. No properties needed or mentioned— outer scene. Men and women crossing the stage as in Scene 2. The bed in Scene 3 is not needed in any way in the action, and the fact that it is on the stage indicates that it could easily be shown and was thought necessary to the setting.

Mayor of Queensborough, ACT V, SCENE 1. A hall. Properties needed—inner scene. (Curtains drawn—doors closed.)
A troop of players enter the hall, enumerate the plays in their
repertory to Simon, and later give one before the Mayor and his
friends. Scene 2. Before the walls. No properties needed
or mentioned—outer scene. (Curtains closed—proscenium
doors and gallery curtains open.) Aurelius and Uther are
besieging a castle, and Vortiger and Horsus are on the walls
defending it. By closing the lower curtains and opening the
upper, a wall scene could follow a room scene without any
loss of time, which was certainly more effective than a long
break in the middle of an act.

Old Law, ACT IV, SCENE 1. Before an inn. Properties
used but not as a regular setting—outer scene. (Curtains
closed—one door open.) The Host says, "Will you drink at
door, gentlemen?" and one replies, "O, the summer air's
best." Here they drink and later "dance a mask." Scene
2. A wood. Properties used—inner scene. (Curtains
drawn—doors open.) Cleanthes says as he enters, "What's
that? O, nothing but the whispering wind breathes through
yon churlish hawthorn." Later "Enter Hippolito from the
Wood." This is a good illustration of an effort to secure
alternation. Scene 1 regularly belongs in a tavern, but as the
next must be an inner with a wood-setting, this was placed
before the door and several lines given up to an apology for
the same.

Before giving the closing full-play illustration of the
continuous act, two peculiar customs in Elizabethan staging
should be noticed. They are so closely connected with the
alternation of scenes that they may be considered at this
point without interrupting the train of thought.

1. *Scenes change with characters on the stage*

We have shown in different ways the rapid changes from
outer to inner scenes and vice versa, but no mention has been
made of the characters during the change. We would suppose
that the dramatists cleared the stage at such times, but in

truth they were very indifferent about this.   Quite often the characters remained on the stage during the opening or closing of the curtains, and were thus suddenly transported from a room to a street—a located to an unlocated scene— without changing their position on the stage.   However, having already met this peculiar custom in Restoration staging, we should naturally expect to find it frequently practised on the Elizabethan stage.

The following examples will serve to illustrate the merging of outer scenes into inner with characters on the stage during the change:

Henry VIII, ACT II, SCENES 2–3.   At the end of a scene between Lord Chamberlaine and the dukes of Norfolk and Suffolk on the outer stage, " Exit Lord Chamberlaine, and the King drawes the Curtaine and sits reading pensively."   The dukes presently enter into conversation with the King, and all are now supposed to be in a private chamber in the palace.

Distresses, ACT VI, SCENES 1–2.   " Enter Leonte, and second Servant."   After a brief scene between the two before the closed curtains, the servant is dismissed, and " Leonte steps to the Arras softly, draws it.   Claramante is discovered sleeping on her Book, her Glass by."

Dido, ACT II, SCENES 1–2.   Aeneas and his lost comrades are talking as if before the walls of Carthage.   The conversation presently turns to the Queen, and at the proper moment one remarks that they are now preparing a banquet in the palace; at this the Queen and her train enter, and the whole stage is apparently a banquet hall.   No change of scene is marked, but, in the light of similar situations in both the Elizabethan and the Restoration drama, the curtains must have drawn at the remark of Sergestus, and the properties in the rear have given the whole stage the appearance of an interior scene.

As illustrations of changes from inner to outer scenes without clearing the stage, the following examples may be given:

Lust's Dominion, ACT I, SCENES 1–2.   " Enter Queen Mother of Spain with two pages: Eleazar, sitting in a chair, the Curtaine is suddenly drawn."   After a scene between

Eleazar and the Queen, some one is heard knocking at the door, and "Eleazar shuts them in." Alvero enters to Eleazar, and a scene takes place between the two as if in a different place.

Pinner of Wakefield, ACT IV, SCENES 3–4. Jenkins enters a shoemaker's shop, and dares the owner to meet him at "the townes end." The challenge is accepted, and after a certain amount of stage business, during which the curtains must have closed, Jenkins says, "Now we are at the townes end, what say you now?"

Just as in the Restoration the "flats" closed at an exeunt of most of the characters, or, to be more specific, at an "exeunt omnes praeter," leaving one or two alone on the stage to continue the action (See *Tyrannic Love*, V, 2–3, *Duke of Guise*, V, 1–2, and 3–4); so must the curtains often have closed in similar situations in Elizabethan plays:

Fair Maid of the Exchange, ACT II, SCENES 1–2. "Enter Franke. The Cripple at worke." At the close of the scene the Cripple says, "And so farewell, I can no longer stand to talke with you, I have some worke in hand." "Exit." The Shop is the Cripple's regular place of work, is no longer used in the scene, and is not a place to be left open by its owner; therefore, the curtains must have closed at the Cripple's exit, leaving Frank on the outer stage to continue the action.

Wise Woman of Hogsdon, ACT I, SCENES 2–3. "Enter Luce in a Sempsters shop, at worke upon a lac 'd Handkercher, and Joseph a Prentice." Other characters pass along the street before the shop during the scene, but towards the close, all exeunt but 2d Luce, who concludes the act with a soliloquy. The situation here is very similar to that in the previous illustration, and undoubtedly the curtains closed at the exeunt of all the characters but one.

I If You Know not Me, ACT III, SCENES 1–2. At the close of a room scene in which a table, chairs, pen, ink, paper, etc. are used, "Exeunt omnes, praeter Bening." Shortly after this, with Benington soliloquizing alone on the stage, "Enter Clown, Barwick, and Soldiers, leading a goat; his sword drawne."

Trick to Catch the Old-One, ACT IV, SCENES 4–5–6.   After a scene in a room in Hoard's house, "exeunt omnes praeter" Witgood (curtains closed).   As he is soliloquizing here, Joyce appears at her window and throws down a letter to him.   The sixth scene (curtains drawn) is a bed room, and apparently discovered.

There is no way of absolutely proving the point that the curtains closed at these general exeunts, but the fact that the "flats" or curtains closed at these places in similar situations in Restoration plays makes it very probable, in the face of Principles I and II, that such was the method.   If the custom was allowable on the Restoration stage with a much larger proscenium arch and a more elaborate setting, it would certainly be tolerated on the Elizabethan.   For the system of staging in vogue throughout the century, it was a most convenient custom.   During these soliloquies, more or less important to the action, the inner stage could be reset for the next scene.

2. *The curtains used as doors*

Scenes in which characters pretend to pass through a door into a house or into another room were very puzzling to me, until I detected the use of "flats" as doors in the Restoration. The situations are the same in the plays of both periods, and in all probability this custom was simply continued from the earlier.   Instead of the "flats" being drawn at a command to open the door, the curtains parted, and in both cases the characters found themselves in another room.   The curtains before 1660 were only about half as high as those after that date, and they would evidently be more appropriate for a door than the long, sweeping curtains or full-sized "flats" of the Restoration.   The following examples will serve to illustrate this use of the curtains:

I   If You Know not Me, ACT I, SCENES 3–4. Scene 3 is before Elizabeth's chamber.   "Enter Tame and Shandoyse, with Souldiers, drum, &c."   They demand admittance to the Princess, but her maid reports, "Her Grace intreats you but to stay till morne, and then your message shall be heard at full"; as she offers to return with their message, Tame says, "It shall not need—Presse after her my Lord." At this they are in the presence of Elizabeth, whose first words are, "We are not pleased with your intrusion, lords." The situation here is very similar to that in *Love for Love*, IV, 5–6 ("Mr. Scandal is with him, Sir; I 'll knock at the door. Goes to the Scene which opens") only the dramatists had not yet learned to use explicit stage directions. As the men pretended to crowd into Elizabeth's chamber, the curtains drew, and the whole stage became her bed room.

I Fair Maid of the West, ACT I, SCENES 1–2. Spencer and Goodlack have come to "the old house,"—the inn which Bess keeps. After a short dialogue, Spencer says "Come let 's enter." With the direction, "Enter 2. Drawers," the scene changes to the interior of the inn. The first drawer says, "You are welcome Gentlemen." Just as in the Restoration, the curtains must have drawn at the last words of Spencer, and the two, without passing off the stage, found themselves in a room in the inn.

Witches of Lancashire, ACT IV, SCENES 1–2. The witches dance across the stage, leaving Robin in a maze at their last words. Presently he says, "What place is this? It looks like an old barne: ile peep in at some cranny or other, and try if I can see what they are doing. Such a bevy of beldames did I never behold; and cramming like so many Cormorants: Marry choke you with a mischiefe." At this, without a break in the text, the witches are at their feast before us, and Robin stands looking on. There is no remark here like "the Presence opens" (in *Duke of Guise*, III, 1) as we pass from one scene to the other, but most likely Robin's peeping in at the cranny was a signal to draw the curtains for the second scene.

After all, these long-since forgotten customs are but special forms of the alternation of outer and inner scenes. They are, however, very important in the system, and without a knowledge of them the action would often seem to halt between the scenes. With the main features of the principle of the continuous act now before us we may turn to the closing full-play illustration.

I If You Know not Me, ACT I, SCENE 1. Unlocated place. Outer scene. Curtains closed—doors open—no properties—action on outer stage. The lords enter two by two, and after a few remarks pass out to "Attend the Queene into the presence." Scene 2. Council chamber. Inner scene. Curtains drawn—doors closed—throne, etc. on the inner stage—action on both stages. The Queen says, "We are instated in our Brothers throne, . . . here may we sit secure. Our heart is joyful, lords, our peace is pure." At the close of the scene Philip's arrival in England is announced, and Mary replies that she will meet him "on the mid way." Scene 3. Before Elizabeth's chamber. Outer scene. Curtains closed—no properties—action on the outer stage. The lords have just arrived for the Princess, and demand "admittance to her presence." Scene 4. Elizabeth's chamber. Inner scene. Curtains drawn—doors closed—room properties on the inner stage—action on both stages. Elizabeth, "in her bed," receives the orders "to appeare at Westminster."

ACT II, SCENE 1. A road. Outer scene. Curtains closed—doors open—no properties—action on the outer stage. Mary and Philip meet "on the mid way," "in the face of Heaven, and broad eye of all the multitude;" after a short scene they go off for the wedding ceremonies. Scene 2. A room. Inner scene. Curtains drawn—doors closed—room properties on the inner stage—action on both stages. The lords have come to examine Elizabeth; "They sit: she kneels." Scene 3. Before Elizabeth's chamber. Outer scene. Curtains closed—doors open—no properties—action on the outer stage. "Enter three white-cote Souldiers, with a jacke of beere" "1. . . . Here we must watch till morning, and then carry the Princesse to the Tower." Scene 4. Before the door of the prison. Outer scene. Curtains closed—one door closed—no properties—action on the outer stage. Elizabeth passes to her cell in the Tower.

ACT III, SCENE 1. Presence chamber. Inner scene Curtains drawn—room properties on the inner stage—action on both stages. The first part of the scene is a dumb show with the King, Queen, lords, and ladies present; "Sussex delivers a petition to the King." Scene 2. Same as Scene 4 in Act II. Outer scene. Scene 3. A room in the Tower. Inner scene. Curtains drawn—doors closed—room properties on the inner stage—action on both stages. The lords enter to Elizabeth with the message that she is to be transferred to the home of Beningfield. Scene 4. A road. Outer scene. Curtains closed—doors open—no properties—action on the outer stage. The people are lined up along the way to see the Princess as she passes. When she appears, Gage says, "These are the townesmen of the country, gather 'd here to greet your Grace, hearing you past this way." Scene 5. A room. Inner scene. Curtains drawn—doors closed—room properties on the inner stage—action on both stages. As Benington is taking " off his boots in the chair of state," " The Clowne pulls the chair from under him." Scene 6. A place. Outer scene. Curtains closed—doors open—no properties—action on the outer stage. A duel between an Englishman and a Spaniard.

Act IV, Scene 1. A room. Inner scene. Curtains drawn —doors closed—room properties on the inner stage—action on both stages. The Princess writes a letter to Mary, and afterwards falls asleep in her chair. Scene 2. A place. Outer scene. Curtains closed—doors open—no properties—action on the outer stage. "Enter Clown, Barwick, and Soldiers, leading a goat: his sword drawne." Scene 3. A council chamber. Inner scene. Curtains drawn—doors closed— room properties on the inner stage—action on both stages. "Philip. Our Chancellor, lords. This is our sealing day: This our States business.—Is our signet there?" Scene 4. A place. Outer scene. Curtains closed—doors open—no properties—action on the outer stage. "Clown. Whither go you so fast, Mistriss Clarentia? Clar. A milking." Scene 5. "Near the Court." Outer scene. Curtains closed— doors open—no properties—action on the outer stage. Elizabeth is waiting to be admitted to the Queen. Scene 6. Presence chamber. Inner scene. Curtains drawn—doors closed—room properties on the inner stage—action on both stages. The Princess is admitted to the Queen, and pardoned by her. Scene 7. A place. Outer scene. Curtains closed—

doors open—no properties—action on the outer stage.   Gage and Clarentia in conversation.

Act V. Scene 1. A room in the court. Inner scene. Curtains drawn—doors closed—room properties on the inner stage —action on both stages.   The first part of the scene is a dumb show; Philip takes his leave of Mary to return to Spain. Scene 2.   In the gallery. Lower curtains closed—gallery curtains drawn—properties and action in the gallery.   Elizabeth receives the news of her election. Scene 3. Presence chamber. Inner scene. Curtains drawn—doors closed— room properties on the inner stage—action on both stages. "Enter foure Trumpeters: . . . The Queene takes state." Elizabeth is crowned Queen of England. Scene 4. A place. Outer scene. Curtains closed—doors open—no properties— action on the outer stage. The mayor of London meets the procession on its way to London.

Did time and space allow, I would outline in a similar way, showing the continuation of the action throughout the act, all of Heywood's plays, but as anyone who examines them can see, it would be simply a repetition of the illustration already given. The omnipresence of the principle of the continuous act in the drama of the seventeenth century shows that the playwrights must have regarded it as a very important law of staging.   Of course, it was not always observed; there are frequent instances in the plays where two differently propertied scenes come together, which must have necessitated some delay in the action, but perhaps they are not more than sufficient to prove the rule.   And in this connection it should be noticed that violations of this principle, as indeed of all the principles of Elizabethan staging, will be found in the greatest number among the more or less crude anonymous plays.   In fact, the principle of the continuous act is as much in use to-day as ever; only the method of securing it is different.   Instead of the alternation and succession of many scenes, there is now the continuation of one scene throughout the act.

Such are the main principles of Elizabethan staging. Collected together for the sake of clearness, they are as follows: I. The properties of a regular setting were located on the

9

inner stage and changed for a new setting either during an act-division or during the playing of a scene on the outer stage. II. When the curtains were closed, the space before them was a stage in itself; when the curtains were drawn, the outer and inner stages became one, and the properties on the inner gave the setting for the whole. III. By means of the alternation of outer and inner scenes, and the succession of outer as well as certain inner scenes, the action in an act, regardless of the number of scenes, was practically continuous from the beginning to the end.

On comparing Chapters IV and V, we find that the majority of the laws of Elizabethan staging survived throughout the seventeenth century. But were these principles as much at home on the stage after 1660 as before? No. A passing reflection on their perfect adaptability to the Shaksperian stage, and their succeeding history, will show this: 1. As there was no painted scenery, the outer scenes needed no location and the inner required only a classification into room scenes, forest scenes, etc. 2. The curtains were only about twelve feet high, and could therefore be opened and closed at any time with little disturbance to the action. 3. The properties being few and plain, a change from an inner to an outer scene could take place without marked contrast or disappointment. 4. The two stages were of the proper proportionate size,—the outer large, and projecting well into the audience, and the inner, shallow and wide, and extending across the entire visible rear of the outer. The advantage of this arrangement of the stage was very great: First, when the curtains were closed, the outer stage was sufficient in size and appearance for any unpropertied scene; when the curtains were drawn, the properties across the rear gave the whole platform the appearance of a set stage. Second, the outer stage by its location and size being the main place for the action, the curtains could open or close at any point without seriously disturbing the performance or changing the position of the action on the stage,—only in the one case, all the properties being cut off, the scene was a street or any unlocated place; while in the other, the properties

PLATE 13.—COURT STAGE IN THE RUBENS ROOM, WINDSOR CASTLE, 1848

being visible in the rear, the whole stage was a room, a forest, or what not.

The introduction of scenery gave the first fatal blow to the old system. With it came also more elaborate staging, which tended to increase the size of the inner stage and importance of set scenes, and to diminish the dimensions of the outer stage and the popularity of unpropertied scenes. Under these conditions there was a marked contrast between the two kinds of scenes: the one was in a fairly realistic setting, the other on a bare stage; the one was removed and illusive, the other prominent and unsupported by properties. For these and other reasons the outer scenes grew less and less in number and importance, and finally gave way to the one-scene act. The outer stage being now no longer needed, the picture frame stage gained an easy victory and soon established itself in all the theaters. The long persistence of the old principles of staging was due to their firm establishment in the English drama. Even after the new system had been established, the old was still continued on a temporarily constructed outer-inner stage, and may still be seen in this manner to-day, though it has long since become a creed outworn.

CHAPTER VI

SHAKSPERIAN METHOD OF STAGE PRESENTATION
(*Continued*)

SPECIAL FEATURES OF SHAKSPERIAN STAGING, ETC.

IN our discussion thus far we have for the sake of clearness confined ourselves to the main principles of Shaksperian staging. There are still a number of points directly or otherwise connected with these laws which need some explanation. These questions will now be taken up one after the other and briefly discussed.

I. USE OF THE UPPER STAGE

The use of the gallery, balcony windows, and "hut" did not necessitate any new principles of staging. These parts were employed generally in connection with the lower stages, and were brought into service in some plays and not in others. They might be called extra fixtures which the dramatist always had at his disposal when he wished to bring in certain kinds of situations. In Chapter III the working of these parts was necessarily discussed in proving their presence; therefore, only a summary is needed here. The gallery served chiefly as the walls of a city, fort, or prison, but occasionally, especially after 1600, as a prison or a place of temporary confinement, an auditorium for the stage audience in a play within a play, a higher point of observation or the upper deck of a ship, and a gallery or room of a house. The balcony windows were brought into service in all scenes calling for a second-story window. Their being comparatively small and commanding a view of the whole stage made them a convenient place for observing or overhearing any action on the lower stage. Their main use, however, was to provide a means for carrying out in a realistic manner the many secret-courtship scenes, of which the one in *Romeo and Juliet* is a typical example. The "hut" furnished a place for concealing both the machinery used in lowering and raising a body, and the characters and vehicles taking part in the action, before the decension and after the ascension.

It may at first thought seem strange that the gallery did not form a more important factor in keeping the action in progress during the act. It was of course occasionally used for an entire scene, as in *I If You Know not Me*, V, 2, but it never became a regular cog in the wheel of the continuous act. The reason for this is threefold: first, the action in the gallery must always be confined to this comparatively small rear space, while that on the inner stage has the liberty of the whole lower platform; second, the lower stage would naturally be considered the earth surface or ground floor, and the gallery any elevated position or the second story of a building, which illusion would in itself make the latter inappropriate for many scenes; third, the outer and inner stages were usually sufficient in themselves to keep the action continuous without the aid of the gallery.

The relative unimportance of the gallery in the system of staging is shown by its history. In the early part of the Elizabethan period the many historical plays, with their scenes of besieging cities, storming forts, and scaling walls, called this member of the stage into frequent service. After 1600 the dramatists turned to a study of manners, motives, and passions, and ceased to a great extent to "fight over York and Lancaster's long jars." From this time on the gallery was used less and less, and in the Restoration it disappeared altogether as a separate and permanent fixture. Yet the principles of staging continued all the while unchanged; the same without the time-honored gallery as with it.

II.   SPECIAL SETTINGS

In addition to the regular settings as described in Principle

I, there were also occasionally special settings, in which the properties were located on the outer stage, and placed there and removed in full view of the audience.

A. Setting for a play within a play

In the preparation of a setting for a play within a play, the audience proper was entirely lost sight of and the presence or absence of the stage audience alone considered. The supposed stage manager and hands brought out the properties, perhaps hung up a curtain, and arranged everything, apparently without a thought of the many onlookers in the audience; when all was ready, the signal was given, and the mock assembly entered. The fact that precaution was taken to set the stage out of view of the pretended audience is strong proof in itself that the regular settings were similarly placed with reference to the real audience.

Spanish Tragedy, IV, 3. "Enter Hieronimo; he knocks up the curtaine. Enter the Duke of Castile." "*Cas.* How now, Hieronimo? Wheres your fellows, That you take all this paine? *Hiero.* O sir, it is for the authors credit to look that all things may go well. . . . Bring a chaire and a cushion for the king." "Enter Balthazar with a chaire." Shortly after this, the "King, Vice-Roy, the Duke of Castile, and their traine" enter the gallery to witness the play. Hieronimo, oblivious of the regular audience, hangs up his curtain somewhere on the outer stage, places his dead son behind it—the body being of course in full view of the main auditory, as a kind of prologue to the little play—orders the other properties brought in, and, in short, sets the stage before the King and court enter.[1]

---

[1] All the students, I believe, of the Elizabethan stage are agreed that the mock auditory in the *Spanish Tragedy*, IV, 3, was in the gallery and that the play within the play was on the lower stage. Few, however, give the same interpretation to the stage direction, "he knocks up the curtaine." Dr. Brodmeier says, "Mit diesem Vorhang ist wohl die Verhüllung der Fenster auf der Oberbühne gemeint"; Dr. Wegener thinks the regular stage curtain is implied; etc. The situation seems to me very plain. The King and his train take their seats in the gal-

Tale of a Tub, V, 5. "Enter Tub, followed by two Grooms, with Chairs, &c. and Rosin and his two Boys." "*1 Groom.* Come, give us the great chair for my lady, and set it there: and this for Justice Bramble. *2 Groom.* This for the 'squire my master, on the right-hand." And so on the grooms continue as they place the chairs. In the meantime Tub is hanging his curtain, placing his tub, and arranging for the motions; after everything is ready, he calls to Rosin for a "flourish to the Masque": "Loud Music. Enter Preamble, lady Tub, Turfe, dame Turfe, Pol Martin, Awdrey, Puppy, Wispe, Hugh, Clay; all take their seats."

Gentleman Usher, II, 1. "Enter Bassiolo with servants with Rushes, and a Carpet." . . . "*Bass.* Come strew this room a fresh; spread here this carpet. . . . *Enter Vin* [*centio*] *and Stroz* [*za*]. . . . *Vin.* Who is this throne for pray? *Bass.* For my Lords daughter. . . . *Vin.* 'T will be exceeding fit; and all this roome is passing well preparde; a man would sweare, that all presentments in it would be rare." During the preparation the different actors drop in; one wondering how to wear his clothes, two quarreling over a certain jerkin, and others at a loss to know just when and where to enter. At last all is complete, and Bassiolo calls "Sound Musicke." "Enter Vincentio, Strozza bare, Margaret, Corteza, and Cynanche bearing her traine. After her the duke whispering with Medice, Lasso with Bassiolo, &c."

There was no definite place for the stage audience and the play-within-a-play scene, but the relative importance of the two and the immediate needs of the situation determined the arrangement in each case. In the *Spanish Tragedy*, IV, 3, the King and court were seated in the gallery, and the play was

lery. Hieronimo gives his play on the outer stage,—the inner being invisible from the gallery. At the psychological moment Hieronimo "Shewes his dead sonne." Where was the corpse? It was behind the curtain which Hieronimo hung up at the opening of the scene. He had prepared all this before the others entered. This temporary curtain was perhaps hung just in front of one of the proscenium doors, and the dead body was visible to the majority of the real audience. The sight of it prepared them for the bloody scene which was about to take place.

on the outer stage.   The show was here of greater significance
than the stage auditory, and, more than this, Hieronimo
needed to be provided to some extent against disturbance
in his play of real life and death.   The mock audience in
Wife for a Month, II, 6, having little to do with the action,
found its proper place on the inner stage; while the masque,
being the all-important part of the scene and consisting partly
of ascending and descending, was given on the outer stage.   In
Hamlet, III, 2, the effect on the conscience of the King is the
thing, and, therefore, the stage audience was undoubtedly on
the outer stage, and the mock play on the inner,—in the same
relative position as the scene is played to-day.

B. Setting for a scene of execution

Scenes of execution may be said to constitute another
class of special settings in which the properties were placed on
the outer stage.   Scaffolds in real life were often erected for
the occasion and taken down afterwards; in some cases the
execution took place where the crime was committed, which
condition would require a special preparation for each event.
Therefore, it was only natural in the play world to erect the
scaffold on the outer stage before the audience and to remove
it when the scene was over.   Considerable space was usually
needed for these scenes, and their prominence in the action
called them as near the audience as possible.

II Edward IV, V.   The order had gone forth from the King
that no one should harbor or in any way give relief to Jane
Shore.   Young Aire, whom Jane had befriended when he was
suffering in prison, found her starving in the streets, and gave
her his purse.   As a result he was arraigned before the King,
and sentenced to be hanged "just in the place where he
relieved Shore's wife."   In the next scene the scaffold was
supposedly built at that place, and the death sentence carried out as directed.   Earlier in the play Shore and Stranguidge were sentenced to death: "Enter one bearing a
silver oare before Stranguidge, Shore, and two or three more
pinioned, and two or three with bills and a hangman. . . ."

The while the Hangman prepares, Shore at this speech mounts up the ladder."

Barnavelt, V, 3. Leidenberg has escaped public execution by killing himself. The authorities are not satisfied with this, and therefore to the place where "A Scaffold [is] put out" for Barnavelt, they bring Leidenberg's corpse, set up a gibbet, and hang the body on it; this done, Barnavelt is led in and put to death.

Virgin Martyr, IV, 2–3. The scene is a large hall where Dorothea is to be publicly whipped. "Enter Dorothea, led Prisoner, a Guard attending; a Hangman with Cords, in some ugly Shape, sets up a Pillar in the Middle of the Stage; Sapritius and Theophilus sit, Angelo by her." One after another applies the rod to the victim, but in the end the Governor, not being satisfied with the torture, gives orders for her execution. In the next scene the scaffold is prepared, and Dorothea meets her death.

There are still other classes of special settings, but an enumeration of them is not necessary. The two already given explain the nature of such scenes, and offer a key to all similar situations. The main thing to be noticed is that special settings are in no way incongruous, nor do they conflict with any of the principles of Elizabethan staging.

III. PROPERTIES MOVED FORWARD AND NEW ONES ADDED AFTER THE SCENE OPENS

According to Principle I, the properties of a regular setting were located on the inner stage, and according to Principle II, the properties on this rear space gave the setting for the whole stage. If the properties were altars or tombs, the whole platform became a church; if they were chairs, tables, etc., the stage took the appearance of a room. When the scene was once before the audience, some or all of the properties could be moved anywhere about the church or the room, or other furniture of the same class added, without in any manner violating the old-time principle of congruity. Under these conditions properties were very often moved forward, and others of a similar nature brought on. This was due to the fact that the action was always carried down as near the audience as possible, and with it occasionally had to come certain properties. The same state of affairs is noticed in the Restoration; for example, in *The Enchanted Island*, V, 1: "Hippolito discovered on a Couch, Dorinda by him." After a few lines, "She draws the Chair nearer to the audience." While it is manifestly impossible and impracticable to attempt to state the manipulation of the properties on the stage in every Elizabethan scene, yet a few general classes of set-forward and added properties may be briefly treated for the sake of illustrating the general custom in such situations.

A. Small properties moved forward and added according to orders

There are frequent instances of one character's ordering another to place a table, chairs, or stools at some convenient place for him. In many cases it is quite probable that this convenient place was the outer stage, and that these directions were little more than an excuse to get the properties and the accompanying action nearer the audience. Instead of a spoken direction, doubtless a look or nod often served the same purpose, and the servant who placed the property forward would see that it was removed when no longer needed.

Royal King and Loyal Subject, III, 4. "Sound, enter the King, Prince, Princesse, all the Lords, the Queene, &c." After a few words are spoken, the King says, "Lords, and the rest forbeare us till we call, a chaire first, and another for our Queene."

City Madam, I, 3. The scene opens in Rich's counting house. Sir John says to his debtors, "What would you have me do?" and apparently to one of his servants, "reach me a Chair."

Phoenix, III, 1. Latronello and Fucato enter Justice Falso's room with the news that "Our fellow Furtivio is taken in the action." Fucato says, "They bring him along to your worship; you 're the next justice. Now or never shew yourself a good master, an upright magistrate, and deliver him out of their hands." The honorable judge replies, "Nay, he shall find me—apt enough to do him good, I warrant him. . . . Go shift yourselves into your coats; bring hither a great chair and a little table."

Royal King and Loyal Subject, V, 3. The scene opens with the direction, "Enter Clinton to Earle Chester in his study." After a short dialogue between the two, other characters enter, and it is decided to arraign the Lord Martial in this very room. Clinton says, "Shall we command a Barre, and call a Iury of his Peeres?" It is agreed that they shall, and the following stage direction reads, "A Barre set out. . . . Audley and Bonvile bring him to the Barre as out of his bed, then take their seates."

B. *Banquets brought on*

Very much like the custom of moving and adding smaller properties on a set scene was that of bringing on and removing a banquet during the action. There are instances where the feast was discovered and perhaps not moved forward, as in *The Guardian*, III, 7, but usually it was carried in at the opening of, or during, the scene. An important part of the action often took place around the table, and under this usage the festal board could be placed on the outer stage where it would find ample space and prominence.

City Madam, V, 3. The scene is a room in Sir John's house. As guests are expected, Sir John steps to the door and orders the servants to "set forth the Table: So." "Enter Servants with a rich Banquet."

The Captain, IV, 4. The servant enters in great flustration because the banquet is not yet prepared. He calls out to a maid in an adjoining room, "Why Nell—whiew— *Maid within*. What's the matter? *Enter Maid. Ser.* I pray you heartily, come away, oh, come, come, the Gentleman my Mistris invited, is coming down the street, and the banquet not yet brought out?" "They bring in the Banquet."

C. *Beds brought on and moved forward*

Bed scenes on the Elizabethan stage have been pretty generally misunderstood. This has been due mainly, of course, to an inadequate knowledge of the general custom of moving properties about on the stage, but partly, I think, to ambiguous, and consequently misinterpreted, stage directions. Therefore, before taking up bed scenes, three very common stage directions, "enter," "exit" or "exeunt," and "set out," may be observed.

1. *"Enter"*

The words "enter," "discover," "curtains draw," "scene opens," and various others are used for the opening of a scene; but the one most often found is the first. In fact the word "enter" before one or more of the *dramatis personae* occurs so frequently that it may be said to be the regular opening term. It seems to apply as well to inner scenes, in which the characters were often "discovered," as to outer scenes, in which they regularly entered.

In the Restoration, when a large inner stage was discovered by drawing the curtains, the old Elizabethan opening was still often retained, except that the location of the scene was usually added first: *Friendship in Fashion*, V, 1. "Scene Victoria's Chamber. Enter Victoria." *She Would if She Could*, V, 1. "Sir Oliver's Dining-Room. Table & Carpet. Enter Lady Cockwood." *Constantine the Great*, V, 2. "A Bedchamber. A Bowl and a Dagger on a Table. Enter Constantius and Arius." *Alcibiades*, II, 2. "A Grove adjoining to the Spartan Camps. Enter Timandra and Draxilla." Indeed there are instances far in the eighteenth century where "enter" and "discover" are both used together, which shows the formality of the former. *Clandestine Marriage*, II, 1. "An Anti-Chamber to Lord Ogleby's Bed-Chamber. Table with Chocolate and a small Case of Medicines. Enter Brush, my Lord's Valet-de-Chambre, and Sterling's Chambermaid, discovered."

The term "enter" in Elizabethan plays, being a kind of formal opening to the scene, often led to a strange stage direction. Along with the word "enter" there was occasionally an attempt to depict the appearance of the scene at the opening, which usually shows all too plainly that the first term meant nothing in itself: *The Guardian*, III, 8. "Enter Jolante (with a rich Banquet and Tapers) in a Chair, behind a Curtain." She is a woman in perfect health, and in her own dining-room; therefore, this is simply a discovered scene with "enter" as a formal opening. *'T is Pity She's a Whore*, III, 6. "Enter the Friar in his study, sitting in a Chayre, Annabella kneeling and whispering to him, a Table before them and wax lights." *Pinner of Wakefield*, IV, 3. "Enter a Shoomaker sitting upon the stage at work." *Valentinian*, II, 1. "Enter the Emmperour, Maximus, Licinius, Proculus, Chilax, as at Dice." They are in the midst of a game, and continue to throw the dice for a short time after the scene opens. *Wise Woman of Hogsdon*, I, 2. "Enter Luce in a Sempsters shop, at worke upon a lac'd Handkercher, and Joseph a Prentice."

Perhaps a still better example of the formal use of the word "enter" is the following: *Sophonisba*, II, 1. "Whil'st the musicke for the first Act sounds, Hanno, Carthalo, Bytheas, Gelosso, enter: they place themselves to counsell; Gisco, the impoisoner, waiting on them; Hanno, Carthalo, and Bytheas setting their hands to a writing, which being offered to Gelosso, he denies his hand, and, as much offended, impatiently starts up and speaks. Enter Gelosso, Hanno, Bytheas, Carthelo. *Gel.* My hand? my hand? rot first: wither in aged shame," etc. The last "enter" before the four *dramatis personæ* is not needed at all; the characters are already on the stage.

With a conception of the meaningless use of "enter" in some situations, we are able to understand certain very strange stage directions in bed scenes:

Court Beggar, IV, 3. "Enter Frederick in a Doctors habit, Gabriel with two swords under his cloake, Ferdinand upon a Bed bound, and held down by servants." An entry of this kind, some carrying a bed and others holding the man down upon it, would be truly ridiculous. The word "enter" is simply here according to custom, and the scene is a regularly discovered one.

Monsieur Thomas, III, 1. "Enter Frank sick, Physicians, and an Apothecary." The first physician shouts, "Clap on the Cataplasm." As Frank remonstrates, the second physician says, "pray keep your arms in, the air is raw, and ministers much evil." The whole scene shows clearly that Frank was lying abed in his own room, and that there was no need of an entry at the opening.

By this discussion I do not mean to imply that every bed scene introduced by "enter" was a discovered one, any more than that all scenes before which the word occurs were inner scenes, but simply that every case of this kind must be judged as discovered or not by the situation and not by the term "enter."

2. "Exit" and "exeunt"

"Exit" and "exeunt" are the regular terms in Elizabethan plays—so far as there are any directions at all—for marking the close of a scene and act. They denote the conclusion of an inner scene as well as an outer, and therefore the kind of scene which they follow can never be determined by them alone.

This same custom still prevailed to a great extent in the Restoration. Many of the acts which close with a well set scene, or with one in which dead bodies are left on the stage, end simply with "exit" or "exeunt." While there may be frequent mention throughout the act of closing the scenes or drawing the curtains, the act itself usually closes with the long established words. In *Venice Preserved* both the new and the old method of marking the close are used. The last scene, in which Pierre and Jaffeir die on the scaffold and Belvidera by her own hands, ends with "Curtain falls. Exeunt omnes."

3 "Set out"

The term "set out" has generally been taken to mean

only one thing,—the placing of properties on the outer stage; but, so far as I can see, there is no ground for such a limited interpretation. It was, of course, often used for moving properties forward or placing them on the front stage, but may it not have been used also for setting properties on the inner stage with the curtains closed? There is often nothing in the text to indicate the part of the stage on which the properties were placed, and I have already shown that the regular settings were always behind the line of the curtains. It, therefore, seems to me more than probable that the term "set out," when referring to a regular setting, signified the placing of properties on the inner stage behind closed curtains.

No one seriously doubts that in the Restoration the regular settings were on the inner stage, and yet this stage direction is frequently found. For example: *Amboyna*, V, 1. "A Table set out. Enter Harman," etc. *Spanish Friar*, II, 3. "Scene, a Chamber, A Table and Wine set out. Enter Lorenzo." *Conquest of China by the Tartars*, V, 2. "The Palace. A Table and Chaires set out, with Pen, Ink, and Paper." If "set out" in these plays refers to the settings on the inner stage, why may not this term in such Elizabethan plays as the following have the same significance: *I Fair Maid of the West*, IV, 2. "Enter Besse, Mayor, Alderman, Clem. A table set out, and stools." *Platonic Lovers*, II, 1. "Enter Ariola, Rosella, with Tapers. A Table with Night-linen set out." *Platonic Lovers*, IV, 1. "Enter Theander, Eurithea, a Table, Stools, and Lights set out." *Renegado*, II, 4. "A Table set forth, Jewels and Bags upon it."

Very similar to "set out" for tables, chairs, etc., are the phrases, "thrust out," "put forth," "thrust forth," used in connection with beds. It is, therefore, probable that these directions, also, occasionally signified nothing more than the particular position of the bed on the inner stage or the placing of it there while the curtains were closed.

These and all other stage directions were sufficiently intelligible to an Elizabethan. Being familiar with the general customs of staging, he did not read the stage directions literally, but interpreted them in all cases according to the immediate needs of the situation. And the same knowledge must be brought to bear upon them to-day; an understanding of Elizabethan staging is necessary for a proper interpretation of the old stage directions.

With this precaution against ambiguous stage directions, we may now take up the topic which heads this section,—beds brought on and moved forward. For the sake of clearness we shall study the subject under two headings, beds in indoor scenes and beds in outdoor scenes.

1. *Beds in indoor scenes*

The Elizabethan plays are full of situations in which a bed, couch, or chair is "thrust forth," "drawn forth," "put out," "drawn out," "put forth," "carried in," "brought in," etc. The explanation of this old custom has already been implied in the previous sections. When the curtains were drawn revealing room furniture on the inner stage, the whole platform became a chamber. A couch standing in the rear when the scene opened could easily be moved forward and drawn back at the close; and similarly a bed could be drawn from an adjoining room and placed on any part of the stage. Beds, couches, and chairs were all used for reclining purposes, but it is likely that in most cases where they were moved about the two latter were generally employed. A couch was a very movable piece of furniture, and carrying it from one room to another, or moving it around in the same room, seems to have been a very conventional thing. For example, in *The Roman Actor*, V, 1, Caesar calls out, "Bring my Couch there: *Enter with Couch*. A sudden but a secure Drowsiness invites me to repose myself."

There are scenes in which the bed was not necessarily used by any of the characters; and others in which the characters on the bed played little part in the action themselves but were there to create the desired effect on the others. As illustrations of the former case: *Caesar and Pompey*, IV, 1. "Porcius in haste, Marcillius bare, following. Porcius discovers a bed, and a sword hanging by it which he takes downe."

Wit without Money, V, 4. Some one is knocking at the door for admittance, and Valentine says, "fling up the bed and let her in." In neither of these scenes was the bed necessarily used; and had there not been a passing mention of it, we should not have known that this piece of furniture was on the stage. It is possible that a bed or couch formed part of the setting of many a scene, even though there is no notice of it in the text.

In the discovered scenes it is always possible that the bed was moved forward during the action, whether or not there are stage directions to this effect. In the following examples, the bed was discovered, and yet drawn in at the close, which shows that it was drawn forward sometime during the action. *Four Plays in One, The Triumph of Love*, Scene 4. "Enter Violante in a Bed; Angelina and Dorothea sitting by her." But at the close Angelina says, "Draw in the Bed nearer the Fire, and silken Rest, tie all thy Cares up." "Exeunt." *Monsieur Thomas*, V, 1. "A Bed discovered with a Blackmoore in it." After the trick is over, Mary says, "Draw in the Bed, Maids, and see it made again."

There are numerous situations in which a character is carried into the presence of another, and may come from an adjoining room, another tent, or from any place. In these cases it is usually stated that they are borne in a chair. For example: *Gentleman Usher*, V, 1. "Enter Strozza, Vincentio, brought in a chaire, Benevenius, Pogio, Cynanche, with a guard, Strozza before & Medice." The Prince has been wounded in a fight with Lord Medice, and is brought into the presence of the King, his father. *King Lear* (folio, 1623), IV, 7. The scene is in and before a tent, where Cordelia is talking with the faithful Kent. At the proper moment, "Enter Lear in a chaire carried by Servants." The child-changed father is brought here that he may awake in the presence of Cordelia. The real object, of course, is that this beautiful, this impressive, this wonderful scene may be played as near the audience as possible. [1]

---

[1] In the quartos no entry is marked for King Lear, and the text is

2. *Beds in outdoor scenes*

In addition to a bed, couch, or chair being used in connection with a room, there are instances where it was carried out into a yard or street. These cases, however, are always provided for by the needs of the situation: *II Edward IV*, III, 4. "Enter M. Blage & her two men, bringing in Shoar alias Floud, in a chaire, his arme bleeding apace." The scene shows that they are before a house, but the first line gives the reason for their carrying him to this place: "So set him here awhile, where is more aire." *Wife for a Month*, IV, 1. "Enter Alphonso, carried on a Couch by two Fryars." The first words of Alphonso explain why he is carried out of the monastery in this fashion:

> "Give me more air, air, more air, blow, blow,
> Open thou Eastern Gate, and blow upon me,
> Distill thy cold dews, O thou icy Moon,
> And Rivers run through my afflicted spirit."

Our study of bed scenes cannot be exhaustive, but only illustrative. It seems, however, that sufficient has been said to throw light on all such scenes. In general, the situation seems to be this: in a room scene a bed could be brought on and placed anywhere on the stage, or one already there moved to any part of the room; in all other bed scenes the presence of this property is explained by the situation.

The list of special features and minor points of Elizabethan staging could be extended indefinitely, but perhaps it has been continued far enough. To summarize it as it stands: 1. The gallery, balcony windows, and "hut" were in a sense extra fixtures, which were always at the disposal of the dramatist whenever he wished to use them. A sufficient summary of the function of these parts was given at the opening of the chapter. 2. There were certain settings, here termed special settings, which were located on the outer stage,

---

slightly different from that of the folios. This may mean that in the early years of the play, Lear was "discovered" on the inner stage, and perhaps moved forward during the scene; but it is very probable that it signifies nothing more than that this bit of "business" was omitted in the quartos.

and placed there and removed in full view of the audience. Two of these are (1) a setting for a play within a play, and (2) a setting for a scene of execution. When properly understood, this "business" is sufficiently consistent. 3. When a scene was once before the audience, properties were moved about on the stage and new ones added: first, small properties were moved forward and added according to orders; second, banquets were brought on and removed; third, beds were brought on and moved forward. This movement of properties was reasonably congruous, because it was not the placing of a setting on the stage but merely the rearranging of one already there.

With this discussion of special features, etc., our study of the Shaksperian stage ends. The main conclusions which we have reached in the essay may be summarized as follows: The liturgical play was performed on *sedes* and *plateae* arranged down the nave and choir of the church; the *sedes* were mainly for the propertied and located scenes, and the *plateae* for the unpropertied and unlocated ones. When the liturgical play of the clergy became the miracles and moralities of the laity, the old form of stage was still retained; the *sedes* and *plateae* of the church were simply transferred to the market-place and guild-hall. In the interludes and shorter moralities the same two classes of stages were used, but only one class— either a *sedes* or a *platea*—could be employed in a play. The Elizabethan stage, consisting of an outer and an inner stage separated by a curtain, two proscenium doors, two balcony windows, a gallery, and a "heavens," was little more than a union of the old *sedes* and *plateae* of the moralities, or the propertied and unpropertied stages of the interludes,—the *sedes* and propertied scaffold being represented by the outer and inner stages combined, and the *platea* and unpropertied scaffold by the outer stage with the curtains closed. The three main principles of Elizabethan staging are the following: I. The properties of a regular setting were located on the inner stage, and changed for a new setting either during an act-division or during the playing of a scene on the outer stage. II. When the curtains were closed, the space before them was a stage in itself; when the curtains were drawn, the outer and inner stages became one, and the properties on the inner gave the setting for the whole. III. By means of the alternation of outer and inner scenes, and the succession of outer as well as certain inner scenes, the action in an act, regardless of the number of scenes, was practically continuous from the beginning to the end.

In conclusion. Shakspere's stage needs no apology. It was a product not unworthy of the great dramatic age. It was plain and somewhat crude, but carefully constructed to meet the needs of the story-like drama. The Elizabethan plays and the Elizabethan people did not call for elaborate stage-settings, but only for sufficient properties to make the playing a representation of real life and not a "public reading." The stage artists were not toiling through the long period of three quarters of a century in ignorance of other stage conditions; different stages and methods of staging were in use on the continent,—yes, even in their very midst, at the court and elsewhere; but the influence of these things is scarcely felt. And only in the declining days of play-writing, after the drama had passed from the thoughtful to the spectacular, did it become necessary to alter the stage and to add those features which had long been knocking for admission.

The stage of Shakspere, I repeat, was plain and simple but fully equipped with all the apparatus necessary to bring out the best that was in his plays. It is sometimes said that the absence of a front curtain made a formal ending in death scenes necessary in order to get the mimic dead off the stage. This may have been so in some plays but not in the majority. The typical Elizabethan tragedy does not deal with the mistakes of a night, but with the long—often life-long—struggles of its hero. Such a play must have an appropriate ending. After the audience has sympathized with a Hamlet or a Brutus through many a scene, it is not satisfied with a sudden death and a drop of the curtain with a thud. It asks to see the body solemnly and reverently borne off the stage as if to its last resting place. And this was the respect which the honored

dead received on the Elizabethan stage. For example, in
The Roman Actor, "Exeunt. A sad Musick, the players
bearing off Paris's body, Caesar and the rest following"; or
in *The Massacre of Paris*, "They march out, with the body of
the King lying on four men's shoulders, with a dead march,
drawing weapons on the ground." Even in the Restoration,
when there was always sufficient space behind the curtain to
conceal the mimic dead, the old custom was occasionally
used: *Cleomenes*. "Take up that Hero's Body, bear it high,
like the Procession of a Deity." . . . "Ex. omnes."
The only satisfying ending I have ever seen to *Hamlet* on the
modern stage was one in which all the characters passed out
before the curtains closed. The King fell on one side of the
stage near Laertes and the Queen on the other. As Hamlet
felt his end drawing near, he made his way to the throne and
there died in the arms of his faithful friend, Laertes.
Just then a march which had previously been heard afar off
drew near and Fortinbras and his men entered. At the request of Horatio, the future King ordered all the dead bodies
to be taken to a public stage, but that of Hamlet to be borne
there like a soldier by four captains; "and for his passage
the soldiers' music and the rites of war [to] speak loudly for
him." While the men were making a temporary litter out
of their shields and spears, the King, Queen, and Laertes were
unnoticeably disposed of. When the bier was ready, the
noble Hamlet was reverently placed on it, the crown laid on
his breast under his folded hands; and lifted high on the
shoulders of the men, he was borne out to the sound of martial music. When the stage was almost clear, the curtains
closed. No more impressive ending could be secured, and
yet the form is Elizabethan.

The story-like drama and the outer-inner stage flourished
together and died together. In their places have come the
episodic drama and the picture-frame stage. Perhaps the
new is as good as the old. We have no King Lears nor Ham-
lets to-day, but this is not because we have the picture-frame
stage, but because we have not the Elizabethan Age with its
crowning dramatic genius, Shakspere.

APPENDIX

AMONG the articles mentioned in the Bibliography there are three doctors' dissertations on the Elizabethan stage: Cecil Brodmeier, *Die Shakespeare-Bühne nach den alten Bühnenanweisungen* (Weimar, 1904). George F. Reynolds, *Some Principles of Elizabethan Staging* (Chicago, 1905). Richard Wegener, *Die Bühneneinrichtung des Shakespeareschen Theaters nach den zeitgenössischen Dramen* (Halle, 1907). Taking them up in the order of their publication, I will give a brief review of each study.

Dr. Brodmeier attempts to explain the Shaksperian stage and staging "nach den alten bühnenanweisungen." He accepts at the outset the stage shown in the DeWitt drawing, but immediately proceeds, without sufficient proof, to add those parts which he thinks are lacking or otherwise out of sight on the Swan stage. He hangs up three sets of large curtains: a middle curtain enclosing the entire space between the two pillars; and two side curtains, one on either side extending from the pillars to the rear wall. Besides adding these hangings, he runs a wall back on both sides of the stage from the outer edge of the two pillars. In this way he forms three main "bühnenfelder,"—the "vorderbühne" in front of the curtain, the "hinterbühne" behind the curtain, and the "oberbühne" or gallery.

In the absence of all proof for such a stage, only a few words need be said in disproof of this reconstruction: 1. It is contrary to all the pictures purporting to represent Elizabethan stages; the Swan has no curtain at all, Kirkman's— the so called Red Bull—has a curtain across a rear door, and the Roxana and Messallina have curtains suspended from the outer edge of the galleries. 2. It is impracticable; it shuts off all rear scenes from the view of a large part of the audience. 3. It does not fall in line with the Restoration stage and with all succeeding English stages. 4. The lines and stage directions in Elizabethan plays flatly contradict such an arrangement.

This form of stage was reconstructed by Dr. Brodmeier to meet the needs of the impossible "alternation theory." According to this theory there was a continuous alternation between scenes on the "vorderbühne" and scenes on the "hinterbühne." All scenes in which the gallery, doors, curtains, or properties were used were played on the back stage. "Clashes" in the alternation of front and back scenes according to these tests are innumerable. A thorough discussion of these "clashes" was given by Dr. Reynolds in the April number of *Modern Philology* for 1905. His article is able, convincing, and final, and nothing needs to be added to it by me. The only question about his article is why he should have spent so much energy in refuting such an impossible idea of the Elizabethan stage and staging. A very few of his illustrations are sufficient to show that Brodmeier's theory on Brodmeier's stage is nonsensical. The stage is impracticable, how could the staging be otherwise? As I have shown in my essay, there were no front and rear scenes, as a rule, but full-stage and outer stage—inner and outer—scenes. Moreover, there was no continuous alternation of the two classes of scenes; one of the requirements of the dramatists was to keep the action in progress during the act, and the alternation of scenes was frequently necessary to meet this demand.

But even Brodmeier's ideas are not half so fatal to a proper understanding of Shakspere's plays as those expressed by Dr. Reynolds in the second half of *Some Principles of Elizabethan Staging*, in *Modern Philology*, June, 1905, and in a recent article, *"Trees" on the Stage of Shakespeare*, in *Modern Philology*, October, 1907. In these studies he lays down the following principle: "This [dramatic] convention [in plays of the Shaksperian theater] allowed the presence upon the

stage of a property or furnishing which was incongruous to the
scene in progress, and which during the scene was thought
of as absent, though standing in plain sight. This incongruity took two forms: either the close juxtaposition upon the
stage of two properties which in reality should have been a
much greater distance apart, or the presence of a property in
a scene where it could never naturally have been; as a tree, for
example, in the midst of a room scene." As an illustration
of this idea, let me quote his clairvoyant description of one
act of an imaginary play:

" The play is one of the romantic dramas so common to the
Elizabethan stage. The scene shifts between a forest and a
desert in Africa, and the city of Rome. Before the performance begins the stage is already set with most of the properties necessary for the production. Near one door stand three
or four trees—as many as the theatre owns and as the stage
space allows. . . . Near the other door are a chair and
table. Between them are twenty or thirty three-legged
stools, and in the background across the front of the rear stage
hangs the closed curtain with a scene from classic story
painted upon it. Across the front of the balcony hangs a
cloth painted to represent a wall, and over the two exposed
doors are respectively the inscriptions 'Rome' and 'Africa.'
On the pillars hangs the title of the play—now, unfortunately,
unknown. Soon the three-legged stools are almost filled
with young gallants. . . . Then the play begins. From
the door marked 'Rome' enter two people in conversation;
the lady Sylvia is, it appears, to be married by her avaricious
guardian to his foolish son. The trees do not disturb us by
their presence—they are unmentioned, and are therefore
unnoticed. As soon as these two are gone, the curtains part,
and the guardian is discovered in his own room bending over
a chest and counting his ward's fortune. He sends for her;
the beautiful boy who plays the part of Sylvia enters and is
ordered to prepare for an immediate marriage. The heiress
protests, but her guardian remains obdurate. Sylvia begins
to prepare for flight as soon as he has left her, and we are soon
aware from her remarks to her maid that the scene has

changed to her chamber, even though she has not left the stage.   Then the curtains, which have been open all this time, though most of the action has been in front of them, now close as she goes out through the door marked 'Rome,' but only to re-enter through 'Africa.'   From her words on 'this forest dark,' 'these mighty trees,' we notice that the scene has again shifted.   But in following Sylvia we did not notice a boy steal through the door into one of the hollow trees.   Now Sylvia appeals to the gods for help, and he steps forth, a wood nymph, and leads her off the stage to find seclusion in the depths of the forest.   The scene returns to the city again, and we hear the guardian directing his son to pursue the escaped maiden.   They sit at the table, and the father very carefully maps out his son's journey.   The foolish boy and his father both leave the stage, but the boy immediately appears through the other door, and is, we learn, lost in the forest.   He hears outlaws coming, and for conceal-ment climbs into the shelter of a leafy tree.   The outlaws discover him, and making him descend, tie him to the tree and leave him alone.   Here his father fortunately finds him, and together they continue the pursuit.   After a short scene in the city again, Sylvia appears, explaining how she has left the forest and taken refuge in this desert.   Here, however, a disguised prince meets her and falls in love with her, intro-ducing in his passionate appeal references to 'these shaggy trees.'

"So the first act closes.   The orchestra plays, and a clown enters and jigs.   But during that amusement a great chair with a canopy above it comes creaking down from the 'heav-ens'   It is the throne of the prince's father, and the young gallants are made to rise and move their stools closer together. More stools are brought in and placed about the throne.   The next scene is obviously to be one of importance and likely to tax the capacity of the stage.   It will, indeed, for the court is to be represented, and the whole strength of the company is required, and the stage with this crowd of actors and specta-tors combined is too small for the trees to be left upon it.   So, since the forest scenes are over and their room is more valuable than their presence, they are taken through the door into the storeroom. With their disappearance our interest in the performance ends, and we leave it to work itself out in the only too well-known way to its happy conclusion."[1]

Here is an unmistakeable picture of an incongruous stage. Tables, chairs, trees, bushes, thrones, etc. are all crowded on one platform at the same time. Trees or what not are carried off and other properties brought on in full view of the audience. This is interesting because it is so different from our stage conditions to-day, but is it a word picture of a typical Shaksperian performance? To answer this, we turn to his arguments.

Much of his support for the incongruous stage rests upon his idea that the English people were from early times schooled in such conditions. He remarks at the outset that "instead of its seeming unreasonable and impossible to Englishmen to have incongruous properties on the stage, it was quite an accustomed thing, something they had long been used to— pre-Elizabethan staging exhibited this same incongruity." He does not discuss the staging of the interludes—the immediate predecessors of the regular Elizabethan plays—but centers his attention on the miracles and long moralities. But even here he does not show us one English play in which "a tree stands in the midst of a room scene." One of his principal illustrations of incongruous staging is *Mary Magdalene*. How different the stage of this play is from his conception of the Elizabethan stage may be seen by comparing the drawing opposite page 16 with his word picture in *"Trees" on the Stage of Shakespeare*. But lest my reconstruction of the stage of *Mary Magdalene* be wrong, I will turn to the stage-plan of *The Castle of Perseverance*, about which there can be no mistake. In the center stands the castle with five scaffolds stationed around it—on the north Belial scaffold, on the

[1] G. F. Reynolds, "'Trees' on the Stage of Shakespeare," *Modern Philology*, October, 1907. It may be worth remarking that his arrangement of scenes in this imaginary play is not Elizabethan. On this point see Robert Prolss, *Von den altesten Drucken der Dramen Shakspeares*.

northeast Covetise scaffold, on the east Deus scaffold, on the south Caro scaffold, and on the west Mundus scaffold. Here are six distinct stages, each one having just such scenes as are appropriate to its setting. There is no medley here, no confusion of locations,—*no tree in the midst of a room scene.* The homes represented by the different scaffolds are perhaps closer together than in real life, but a space of forty to fifty feet between each *sedes* is sufficient in this mimic world to keep the localities clearly distinguished. Dr. Reynolds does not mention *The Castle of Perseverance*, though its stage-plan is a corner-stone in pre-Shaksperian staging, but his proof of incongruity from *Mary Magdalene* is overthrown by the diagram accompanying *The Castle*, as the two plays were certainly staged in the same fashion. In short, his arguments for incongruity from the miracles and long moralities amount to little more than a misconception and misappreciation of pre-Elizabethan staging.

Taking up the Elizabethan drama, Dr. Reynolds points out in plays ranging in date of publication from 1584 to 1633, but supposedly written before 1603, a number of incongruities; in eighteen plays one incongruity each, in seven plays two incongruities each, and in nine plays three or more incongruities each. This seems like a goodly number of incongruities, but when we consider that in the extant plays before 1603 there are perhaps a thousand scenes, this number hardly seems sufficient for the establishment of hard and fast principles for the playing of all. But barring this objection, we hasten to examine as many of his illustrations of incongruity as space will permit.

"*Romeo and Juliet* (quarto 2, 1599; 4, undated; folio, 1623), I, 4, 5. Romeo and his friends are at first before the house of Capulet, but with the direction, 'They march about the Stage, and Serving men come forth with their napkins,' the scene changes to the interior of the house." According to the custom in Elizabethan and Restoration staging, which has been fully explained above in Chapters IV–VI, the curtains, which had been closed, were drawn at this point; and with room properties on the inner stage, which doubtless the servants

proceeded hastily to arrange over any part of the stage before
the company entered to the masque, the whole stage took the
appearance of a room in Capulet's house.

"*Dido* (1594), I, 1, l. 120: The scene up to this point is not
definitely located at all, but since it is between Jupiter, Venus,
and Ganymede, one would naturally assume it to be upon
Olympus. It certainly is not in the midst of a wood on the
seashore near Carthage, where the action from that point on
is situated." This is demanding even more than we would
to-day. A sylvan scene is entirely appropriate here for the
gods, and no one takes a thought of its exact location until
Aeneas appears on the stage. We would play the scenes in
the same way on the modern stage.

"*Iron Age* (1632), p. 379: The Greek soldiers are besieging
Troy. 'Now with a soft march enter at this breach,' they say.
'They march softly in at one doore, and presently in [out¹] at
another.' After this direction the scene is near the wooden
horse, which stands within the city." This is very plain.
The audience knows that the horse is inside the walls. After
the soldiers have made their way through the "breach" (one
of the proscenium doors—curtains closed) the curtains draw
revealing the wooden horse, and the men rush out through
the inner stage. The presence of the horse gives the appearance of a scene within the city.

The illustration from the 1604 edition of *Doctor Faustus*
certainly shows one case of incongruous staging if the text is
genuine. But I do not believe this edition is reliable. After
Faustus has entertained the emperor in the palace with
his magic tricks, he says he will walk across "this fair and
pleasant green" to Wittenberg, but just as he utters the last
word, in comes the horse-courser, apparently in Faustus's
study. The 1616 version has not this absurd situation, and,
I believe, comes nearer representing the acting edition.

"*English Traveler* (1633), IV, 3, p. 66: 'Tables and
stools set out; Lights: a Banquet, Wine.' At the end of the

¹ The explanatory *out* is in the wrong place here; it should follow
the first *in* in this stage direction. *In* is regularly used for coming
on the stage and *out* for going off.

banquet all the family retire to their chambers, but a guest, Geraldine, is left to rest on a pallet. He cannot sleep and decides to seek the room of his hostess. 'He goes in at one doore, and comes out at another' (p. 69). The scene, in spite of the continued presence of the pallet, and perhaps of the table, is now plainly in the corridor before the bedroom. He listens at the door, hears voices within, and decides to leave the house." There is no need here for a change of scene. The sleeping room of Mrs. Wincott is just off the large hall-room in which the dialogue between the two men takes place. Perhaps Geraldine went off the inner stage, and returning through one of the proscenium doors, made his way to the other which was supposed to open into the lady's chamber. The position of the proscenium door gave the hero a conspicuous place on the stage for this emotional scene. There is, of course, a possibility that the curtains closed, shutting off all properties, at the exit of Geraldine from the inner stage; and on his return through the proscenium door, the stage presented the appearance of a corridor before the bedroom.

"*George-a-Greene* [*Pinner of Wakefield*] (1599), 11, 1037, 1038. The shoemaker seated at his work sees Jenkins and picks a fight with him, which is to occur at the town's end. 'Come, sir, wil you go to the townes end now sir?' 'I sir, come.' In this interval they are supposed to go. The line continues: 'Now we are at the townes end, what say you now?'" I have already given an explanation of this scene on page 124.

"[*I*] *If You Know not Me You Know Nobody* (1605), p. 224: The scene opens with a great procession. 'Queen takes state'—that is, she ascends her throne; after which she pardons her enemies and oppressors. When this is over, Elizabeth says: 'And now to London, lords, lead on the way.' 'Sennet about the stage in order,' is the following direction. Then the mayor of London meets them, saying, '"I from this citie London," bring gifts.'" The curtains close during the "Sennet about the stage in order," and the throne and all properties being cut off from view, the stage becomes an unlocated place—perhaps the road to London.

Eastward Ho, IV. The succession of scenes in this act is not incongruous when properly understood: Scene 1. Outer scene and gallery. Curtains closed—gallery curtains open—doors open. Slitgut in a tree in the gallery sees "a boat cast away hard by" and a little later a lady shipwrecked at St. Katherine's. Scene 2. Outer scene. All curtains closed—one door closed. A drawer brings Winifred to the tavern, which is entered by the closed proscenium door. Scene 3. Same as Scene 1. Slitgut sees another "a taking up at Wapping now." Scene 4. Outer scene. All curtains closed—doors open. Three shipwrecked men meet. Scene 5. Same as Scene 2. Winifred coming out of the tavern meets her husband. Scene 6. Same as Scene 1. Slitgut completes his mission at Cuckold's Haven and departs. Scene 7. A room in Touchstone's house. Inner scene. Gallery curtains closed—curtains drawn—doors closed—room setting on inner stage—action on both stages. The runaways are brought to justice before Master Golding.

The scenes in *Sapho and Phao* are easily staged if we place Vulcan's shop inside one of the proscenium doors, and represent the cave scenes by drawing the curtains just a little in tent-like fashion. In *Parisitaster* the tree referred to in Acts IV–V was probably not on the stage at all. Its particular kind, location, and appearance are all described, which would be hardly necessary if it was visible to the audience. In *Alphonsus, King of Aragon*, Act III, 2–3, the curtains closed at the exit of the Great Turk, and during the soliloquy of Fausta the inner stage was changed—throne removed and trees set in its place. The chairs mentioned in *I Tamburlaine*, IV, 2, and *Alphonsus, King of Aragon*, II, 1, were, I believe, a kind of carrying-chair or triumphal chariot in which a conqueror was often carried or pulled; and as such would be perfectly in place in outdoor scenes. The carrying-chair is occasionally used to-day in Shaksperian performances. *Old Wives Tale* and *Faery Pastoral* were not written to be played according to the regular method of staging, and must therefore be barred in a study of principles of Elizabethan staging.

In conclusion. Considering the number of extant plays

written before 1603 and the fact that the regular stage was yet in its infancy, we should not be greatly surprised if the scenes which Dr. Reynolds has selected after an examination of "practically every extant play accessible to students, published between 1559 and 1603," were incongruous. But I believe that the majority of these were not incongruous when the Elizabethan stage and its working are properly understood. There were, as we have already said, a great deal of crudity and many incongruities in the Elizabethan drama, but incongruity— "as a tree, for example, in the midst of a room scene"—never existed as a *principle* of either pre-Elizabethan or Elizabethan staging.

Dr. Wegener's thesis is the most thorough study that has heretofore been made on the Elizabethan stage and staging. He has reconstructed a stage not from Shakspere's plays alone nor from the plays of a certain part of the period 1576–1648, but from a complete survey of the Elizabethan drama.

He conceives of three types of stages in regular use in the Elizabethan period,—public, private, and court. For a typical public stage he would make, in the main, but one addition to the De Witt drawing of the Swan theater, namely, the "unterbühne," or understage. He would cut away part of the rear wall, as shown in the Swan picture, between the two doors, and thus reveal a room under the gallery. This extra space, closed and revealed by a curtain suspended from the outer edge of the gallery, would serve as the study in *Lord Cromwell*, *Dr. Faustus*, etc.; as an arbor in *Spanish Tragedy*, *Broken Heart*, etc.; as the cell of a monk in *Friar Bacon and Friar Bungay*, etc.; as a counting room or business room in *Jew of Malta*, etc.; as a schoolroom in *How a Man May Choose a Good Wife from a Bad*, etc.; as a sleeping or sick room in *Witch of Edmonton*, *Giovana and Annabella*, *Broken Heart*, etc.; and as the place for many other similar scenes. On the private stage, that of the Blackfriars in particular, there were the same stage-regions, "hauptbühne," "unterbühne," and "oberbühne," but there was possibly also the important addition of a middle curtain which divided the "hauptbühne" into two parts,—"vorderbühne" and "hinterbühne." This curtain would allow the properties on the rear half of the main stage to be brought on and removed out of sight of the audience; but there would be no playing on the front half during the change, as there were no proscenium doors to this space. The court stage contained a front curtain which completely concealed from the auditory all scene-shifting.

This gradation from the public to the court stage seems at first glance a perfectly natural one, but it leads to a most glaring inconsistency when the staging is considered. On the public stage trees and many other properties were on the "hauptbühne," and were set and removed in full view of the audience; on the private stage, if the middle curtain was used, the majority of the properties were on the "hinterbühne," and therefore changed behind closed curtains; on the court stage all scene-shifting took place behind the front curtain. Some theater-goers witnessed plays on all three stages, and many attended both the Globe and the Blackfriars. Now if incongruity was rife on the public stage—if woods and other settings were hauled on and off before their eyes— why should they demand a curtain at the private and court theaters? Or if they were used to an unseen change at Whitehall and Blackfriars, how could they tolerate the confusion, disturbance, and incongruity of setting and re-setting the stage at the Globe? Gradations of incongruity, gradations of congruity are conceivable, but a sudden change from the one to the other is inconceivable. If the middle-curtain theory is disposed of, and the regular setting on both the public and the private stage is placed on the inner stage, the change in the staging of a play at the Globe and a masque at the court is, in the main, one of degree, not of kind.

Dr. Wegener saw clearly enough that a curtained space was needed on the public stage, but he failed to comprehend the full significance of this "unterbühne." He conceived of it as a special place for the representation of such scenes as schoolrooms, studies, monks' cells, and the like; that is, as a third stage which the dramatist could make use of at any time, just as he could of the "oberbuhne." If my thesis carries any weight, it shows that the inner stage was not a stage in itself, but that it became a part of the outer stage the minute the curtains were drawn. The inner stage extended across the rear of the outer stage, and with its properties gave the whole stage the appearance of a set scene, while in itself it contained little of the important action. In short, it was an ever-present and an all-important factor in the Elizabethan system of staging.

Space does not permit a review of the many shorter articles on the stage, but a few words must be said about a recent article,—*The Elizabethan Stage* by William Archer.[1] This is one of the most original and enlightening articles on the Shaksperian stage that has yet appeared. His conception of the material stage is so nearly like my own that it would be useless to point out the slight differences. Mr. Archer is perhaps the most competent man living to study the Elizabethan stage. As a learned dramatic critic of to-day, he approaches the Elizabethan stage with that special insight and ability which a closet student cannot hope to have. The stage and staging have changed since the days of Shakspere, but the mimic world is still the mimic world; and the deeper the scholar is grounded in the stage of to-day, the better he is qualified to study the stage of yesterday.

[1] *Quarterly Review*, April, 1908, pp. 442–471.

CRITICAL BIBLIOGRAPHY

NOTE.—I do not give a bibliography on the pre-Shaksperian stage. A complete one will be found in the first volume of E. K. Chambers' *Mediaeval Stage*.

Biographical Chronicle of the English Drama, A, 1559–1642. F. G. Fleay. 2 vols. 1891.

Bühne Shakespeares, Zur. W. Bang. Shakespeare Jahrbuch, vol. xl.

Bühneneinrichtung des Shakespeareschen Theaters nach den zeitgenössischen Dramen. Richard Wegener. 1907.

Children of the Chapel at Blackfriars. C. W. Wallace. 1908.

Chronicle History of the London Stage, 1559–1642, A. F. G. Fleay. 1890.

Contemporary Drawing of the Swan Theatre, On a. H. B. Wheatley. New Sh. Soc. Trans., 1887–92.

Dekoration der modernen Bühne in Italien . . . bis zum Schluss des XVI Jahrhunderts, Die. E. Flechsig. 1894.

Development of Shakespeare as a Dramatist, The. G. P. Baker. 1907.

Early French Players in England. W. J. Lawrence. Anglia, vol. xxxii.

Early London Theatres. T. F. Ordish. 1894.

Elizabethan Drama, 1558–1642. F. E. Schelling. 2 vols. 1908.

Elizabethan Stage, The. William Archer. Quarterly Review, April, 1908.

Elizabethan Stage Scenery. Mrs. C. C. Stopes. Fortnightly Review, June, 1907.

Elizabethan Stage Theories. The London Times, November 3, 1905.

England as Seen by a Foreigner. W. B. Rye. 1865.

Englische Komödianten am Hofe des Herzogs Philipp Julius
von Pommern-Wolgast. C. F. Meyer. Shakespeare
Jahrbuch, vol. xxxviii.

Englischen Bühne um 1600, Zur. Carl Grabau. Shakespeare Jahrbuch, vol. xxxviii.

Extracts from the Accounts of the Revels at the Court in the
Reigns of Elizabeth and King James I. Ed. P. Cunningham, Old Sh. Soc., 1842.

First Performance in Shakespeare's Time, A. Herbert W.
Fisher. Atlantic Monthly, March, 1898.

Forgotten Stage Conventionality, A. W. J. Lawrence.
Anglia, vol. xxvi.

Fortune Theatre, The. William Archer. London Tribune,
Oct. 12, 1907. Repr. New Shakespeariana, Oct., 1908;
Shakespeare Jahrbuch, 1908.

Gull's Hornbook, The. Thomas Dekker. 1609. Ed. by G.
F. Nott, 1812.

Hamlet on an Elizabethan Stage. G. P. Baker. Shakespeare
Jahrbuch, vol. xli.

Handbook of London. P. Cunningham. 2 vols. 1849.

Historia Histrionica, an Account of the English Stage.
James Wright. 1699. Repr. in Hazlitt's Dodsley, vol.
xv.

Historical Account of the English Stage. Edmund Malone.
1805.

Historical Novel, The. Brander Matthews. 1901.

History of English Dramatic Literature to the Death of
Queen Anne, A. A. W. Ward. 2d ed. 3 vols. 1899.

History of English Dramatic Poetry to the Time of Shakespeare: and Annals of the Stage to the Restoration.
J. P. Collier. 3 vols. 1831. New ed., 1879.

History of the London Stage and its Famous Players. H.
Barton Baker. 1904.

History of Theatres in London from their first opening in
1576 to their closing in 1642. F. G. Fleay. Royal
Historical Society Transactions, vol. 10.

History of Theatrical Art in Ancient and Modern Times, A.
By Karl Mantzius. With an Introduction by William

Archer. Authorized Translation by Louise von Cossel.
5 vols., 1903–09.

Influence of Theatrical Conditions on Shakespeare, The.
E. E. Hale, Jr. Modern Philology, vol. i.

Kenntnis der altenglischen Bühne, Zur. K. T. Gaedertz. 1888.

Lateinischen Universitäts-Dramen in der Zeit der Königen
Elizabeth, Die. G. B. Churchill and W. Keller. Shakespeare Jahrbuch, vol. xxxiv.

London. Walter Besant. 1892.

London Past and Present. H. B. Wheatley. 3 vols. 1891.

Londoner Theater und Schauspiele im Jahre 1599. G. Binz.
Anglia, vol. xxii.

Midsummer Night's Dream, A. Ed. G. P. Baker. 1895.
Introduction.

Mounting of the Stuart Masques, The. W. J. Lawrence. The
English Illustrated Magazine, November, 1903.

Music in the Elizabethan Theatre. W. J. Lawrence. Shakespeare Jahrbuch, 1908.

Neue Art Shakespeare zu spielen, Eine. A. Brandl.
Deutsche Rundschau, April, 1905.

Neue Shakespeare-Bühne, Eine. Ernst Lepold Stahl. Shakespeare Jahrbuch, 1908.

New History of the English Stage, from the Restoration to
the Liberty of the Theatres, A. P. H. Fitzgerald. 2 vols.
1882.

Nochmals zur Bühne Shakespeares. W. Keller. Shakespeare
Jahrbuch, vol. xl.

Outlines of the Life of Shakespeare. J. O. Halliwell-Phillipps.
2 vols. 9th ed., 1892.

Plays and Poems of William Shakspeare with the Corrections
and Illustrations of Various Commentators. Edmund
Malone. 21 vols. 1821.

Prolegomena zu einer Darstellung der englischen Volksbühne
zur Elizabeth-und Stuart-Zeit nach den alten Bühnen-
Anweisungen. Paul Mönkemeyer. 1905.

Richard II Performed at the University of London by the
Elizabethan Stage Society, Nov. 11, 1899. Athenaeum,
Nov. 18, 1899.

Roscius Anglicanus; or, an Historical Review of the Stage from 1660 to 1706. John Downes. Ed. Joseph Knight, 1886.

Scenischen Formen Shakespeare's, Die. Eugen Kilian. Shakespeare Jahrbuch, vol. xxviii.

Scenischen Formen Shakespeare's in ihrem Verhältnisse zur Bühne seiner Zeit, Ueber die. R. Genée. Shakespeare Jahrbuch, vol. xxvi.

Seeing an Elizabethan Play, and Some Particular Discourse on the Knight of the Burning Pestle, On. 1903.

Shakespeare and His Times. N. Drake. 1817.

Shakespeare and Mr. Barrie: The Tempest: Performance by The Elizabethan Stage Society at the Mansion House, November 5, 1897. The Little Minister: A Play in Four Acts. By J. M. Barrie. . . . Haymarket Theatre, November 6, 1897. G. B. S.[haw]. Saturday Review, London, November 13, 1897.

Shakespeare and the Modern Stage. Sidney Lee. Nineteenth Century, January, 1900.

Shakespeare and the Plastic Stage. John Corbin. Atlantic Monthly, March, 1906.

Shakespeare auf der Modernen Bühne. Eugen Kilian. Shakespeare Jahrbuch, vol. xxxvi.

Shakespeare-Bühne nach den alten Bühnenanweisungen, Die. Cecil Brodmeier. 1904.

Shakespeare in France. J. J. Jusserand. 1898.

Shakespeare on the Stage in the Elizabethan Manner. William Poel. The Times, London, Literary Supplement, June 2, 1905.

Shakespeare's London; a Study of London in the Reign of Queen Elizabeth. T. F. Ordish. 1897.

Shakspere's London. H. T. Stephenson. 1905.

Shakspere's Predecessors in the English Drama. J. A. Symonds. 1884.

Sixteenth Century Playhouse, A. William Archer. Universal Review, June, 1888.

Some Account of the English Stage from the Restoration in 1660 to 1830. J. Genest. 10 vols. 1832.

Some Characteristics of the Elizabethan-Stuart Stage. W. J. Lawrence. Englische Studien, vol. xxxii.

Some Principles of Elizabethan Staging. G. F. Reynolds. Modern Philology, April and June, 1905.

Stage History of Richard III. Alice I. Perry Wood.

Stage of the Globe, The. E. K. Chambers, 1907. (In the Works of William Shakespeare, vol. x.)

Staging of Shakespeare, The. A Defense of the Public Taste. H. Beerbohm Tree. Fortnightly Review, July, 1900.

Staging of Shakespeare, The. A Reply to Mr. Beerbohm Tree. W. Hughes Hallett. Fortnightly Review, September, 1900.

Staging of Shakespeare, The: a Rejoinder. Arthur Dillon. Westminster Review, October, 1900.

Survey of London. John Stow. 1598. Enlarged by A. Munday and J. Strype in 1724.

"Trees" on the Stage of Shakespeare. G. F. Reynolds. Modern Philology, October, 1907.

William Shakespeare. George Brandes. 1896. Translation by William Archer. 2 vols. 1898.

LIST OF PLAYS

NOTE.—I have used in my essay the editions of plays which were accessible to me. Most of the modern editions are found in Columbia University Library, and as a usual thing I have consulted all of them; but in the following list, I give only the edition which I have used most frequently. I have not had access to many quartos and folios, and have verified only a few of the most important quotations. Some quotations must therefore be wrong. I have, however, used all the care and judgment possible in selecting them, and I do not believe that many of them will be found to differ materially from the quartos and folios.

In this list the following abbreviations are used: Anon. = anonymous; W. = written; A. = acted; S.R. = entered in the Stationers' Register; P. = published; L. = Licensed.

Adam. Anon. MS. "belongs to the twelfth or the thirteenth century." Excerpts from the stage directions are found in E. K. Chambers, The Mediaeval Stage, pp. 80–81.

Albion Knight. Anon. A. *c.* 1560. S.R. 1565–6. Anonymous Plays, Second Series, J. S. Farmer, 1906.

Alcibiades. Thomas Otway. A. 1675. The Works of Mr. Thomas Otway; in 3 Volumes Consisting of His Plays, Poems, and Letters, 1758. Vol. i.

Alphonsus, King of Aragon. Robert Greene. A. before 1589. P. 1599. The Plays and Poems of Robert Greene, J. Churton Collins. 2 vols., 1905. Vol. i.

Alphonsus, King of Germany. George Chapman(?) A. 1592 (?). P. 1654. The Comedies and Tragedies of George Chapman, Now First Collected, etc., 3 vols., 1873. Vol. iii.

Amboyna. John Dryden. A. 1673. The Comedies, Tragedies, and Operas. Written by Mr. John Dryden, Esq.; now first collected together, and corrected from the originals, 1701.

Amphitryon. John Dryden. A. 1690. The edition of Dryden's Works quoted above.

Amphitryon. Plautus. The Comedies of Plautus, literally translated into English prose, with notes, by H. T. Riley. 2 vols., 1902. Vol. ii.

Andria. Terence. The Comedies of Terence and the Fables of Phaedrus, literally translated into English prose, by H. T. Riley, 1906.

II Antonio and Mellida. John Marston. A. 1600. P. 1602. The Works of John Marston, A. H. Bullen. 3 vols., 1887. Vol. i.

Appius and Virginia. R. Bower. W. c. 1563(?). S.R. 1567-8. P. 1575. Anonymous Plays, Fourth Series, J. S. Farmer, 1908.

Author's Farce. Henry Fielding. A. 1730. The Theatre, 1730. Vol. xiv.

Barnavelt. Fletcher and Massinger. A. 1619. Old English Plays, A. H. Bullen. 4 vols., 1882-5. Vol. ii.

Bartholomew Fair. Ben Jonson. A. 1614. P. 1631. The Works of Mr. Ben Jonson, Gifford-Cunningham. 3 vols. 1904. Vol. ii.

Beggar's Bush. Fletcher and Massinger. A. c. 1615. P. 1647. The Works of Mr. Francis Beaumont, and Mr. John Fletcher, in ten Volumes, by the Late Mr. Theobald, Mr. Seward of Eyam in Derbyshire, and Mr. Sympson of Gainsborough, 1750. Vol. iv.

Blessed Sacrament. Anon. MS. of date about 1461. Specimens of the Pre-Shaksperean Drama, J. M. Manly. 2 vols., 1904. Vol. ii.

Bloody Brother. Fletcher, Jonson(?), and others. W. after 1624. A. 1637. S.R. 1639. P. 1640. The edition used in Beggar's Bush. Vol. v.

Blurt Master Constable. Thomas Middleton. A. 1600-1. P. 1602. The Works of Thomas Middleton, A. H. Bullen. 8 vols, 1885. Vol. i.

Bondsman. Philip Massinger. L. 1623. S.R. 1624. P. 1639. The Dramatic Works of Philip Massinger, complete in four volumes, by J. M. Mason, 1779. Vol. ii.

Brazen Age. Thomas Heywood. P. 1613. The Dramatic Works of Thomas Heywood, with notes and a memoir of the author. 6 vols., 1874. Vol. iii.

Broken Heart. John Ford. A. c. 1629. P. 1633. The Works of John Ford, W. Gifford. 2 vols., 1826. Vol. i.

Bussy d'Ambois. George Chapman. A. 1604(?). P. 1607. The edition of Chapman's Works quoted above. Vol. ii.

Calisto and Meliboea. Anon. P. 1630. Anonymous Plays, First Series, J. S. Farmer, 1905.

Cambises. Thomas Preston. S.R. 1569-70. Dodsley's Old English Plays, W. C. Hazlitt. 15 vols., 1876. Vol. iv.

Cambyses. Elkanah Settle. A. 1666. Quarto, 1671.

Captain. (Beaumont and) Fletcher. A. 1612-13. P. 1647. The Works of Francis Beaumont and John Fletcher, A. Glover and A. R. Waller. 11 vols., 1905- (edition in progress). Vol. v.

Castle of Perseverance. Anon. MS. written during the reign of Edward IV. (1461-1483). Macro Plays, F. J. Furnivall and A. W. Pollard, in the Early English Text Society, Extra Series, Vol. xci.

Chances. (Beaumont and) Fletcher. A. 1615(?). P. 1647. The edition of Beaumont and Fletcher's Works by Glover and Waller already quoted. Vol. iv.

Chaste Maid. Thomas Middleton. A. 1612(?). P. 1630. The edition of Middleton's Works already quoted. Vol. v.

Chester Plays. Anon. Five MSS. of dates 1591-1607. Chester plays, ed. by Thomas Wright, 1847, for the Shakespeare Society.

City Madam. Philip Massinger. W. c. 1619(?). A. 1632. P. 1653. The edition of Massinger's Works already quoted. Vol. iv.

Cleomenes. John Dryden. A. 1692. The edition of Dryden's Works already quoted.

Coelum Britannicum. Thomas Carew. A. 1634. P. 1634. The Works of Sr. William D'Avenant, Kt. Consisting of those which were formerly Printed, and those which he designed for the Press: Now Published out of the Author's Original Copies, 1673.

Conquest of China by the Tartars. Elkanah Settle. A. 1676. Quarto, 1676.

Constantine the Great. Nathaniel Lee. A. 1684. The Works of Mr. Nathaniel Lee, in three Volumes, 1722. Vol. ii.

Court Beggar. Richard Brome. A. 1640(?). P. 1653. The Dramatic Works of Richard Brome, containing fifteen comedies, now first collected in three volumes, 1873. Vol. i.

Cruel Brother. William Davenant. L. 1627. P. 1630. The edition of Davenant's Works already quoted.

Cruelties of the Spaniards. William Davenant. A. 1658. The edition of Davenant's Works already quoted.

David and Bethsabe. George Peele. W. c. 1588. P. 1599. The Works of George Peele, A. H. Bullen. 2 vols., 1888. Vol. ii.

Devil is an Ass. Ben Jonson. A. 1616. P. 1631. The edition of Jonson's Works already quoted. Vol. ii.

Dick of Devonshire. Anon. A. 1625. Old English Plays, A. H. Bullen. Vol. ii.

Dido. Marlowe and Nash. A. 1591. P. 1594. The Works of Christopher Marlowe, Francis Cunningham, 1902.

Digby Plays. Anon. A collection of fifteenth-century plays. The Digby Mysteries, F. J. Furnivall. Edited in 1882 for the New Shakspere Society, and reprinted in 1896 for the E. E. T. S. Extra Series, vol. lxx.

Disobedient Child. Thomas Engelend. W. before 1553(?). A. 1560–61(?). P. c. 1564. The Dramatic Works of Richard Wever and Thomas Engelend, J. S. Farmer, 1905.

Distresses. William Davenant. S.R. 1639. P. 1673. The edition of Davenant's Works already quoted.

Doctor Faustus. Christopher Marlowe. A. 1588. P. 1604. The edition of Marlowe's Works already quoted.

Don Carlos. Thomas Otway. A. 1676. The edition of Otway's Works already quoted. Vol. i.

Downfall of Robert Earl of Huntington. **Anthony Munday.** A. 1598. P. 1601. Hazlitt's Dodsley. Vol. viii.

Duchess of Malfy. John Webster. A. *c.* 1612. P. 1623. The White Devil and The Duchess of Malfy, by John Webster, M. W. Sampson, 1904.

Duke of Guise. Dryden and Lee. A. 1682. The edition of Dryden's Works already quoted.

Eastward Ho. Jonson, Chapman, and Marston. W. 1604–5. P. 1605(?). The edition of Marston's Works already quoted. Vol. iii.

Edward I. George Peele. A. 1590–1(?). P. 1593. The edition of Peele's Works already quoted. Vol. i.

I Edward IV. Thomas Heywood. A. 1594. P. 1600. The edition of Heywood's Works already quoted. Vol. i.

II Edward IV. Thomas Heywood. A. 1594. P. 1600. The edition of Heywood's Works already quoted. Vol. i.

Emperor of the East. Philip Massinger. L. 1631. P. 1632. The edition of Massinger's Works already quoted. Vol. ii.

Empress of Morocco. Elkanah Settle. A. 1671. Quarto, 1687.

Enchanted Island. John Dryden. A. 1667. The edition of Dryden's Works already quoted.

English Traveler. Thomas Heywood. A. *c.* 1627(?). P. 1633. The edition of Heywood's Works already quoted. Vol. iv.

Evening's Love. John Dryden. A. 1668. The edition of Dryden's Works already quoted.

Faery Pastoral. William Percy. W. 1601. P. 1824. Two Plays by William Percy. Ed. by J. Halsewood, 1824, for the Percy Society.

Fair Maid of the Exchange. Thomas Heywood. W. 1602(?). P. 1607. The edition of Heywood's Works already quoted. Vol. ii.

I Fair Maid of the West. Thomas Heywood. W. before 1603(?). P. 1631. The edition of Heywood's Works already quoted. Vol. ii.

Family of Love. Thomas Middleton. A. 1607(?). P. 1608.

The edition of Middleton's Works already quoted. Vol.
iii.

Fatal Marriage. Thomas Southerne. A. 1694. Plays Written by Thomas Southerne, Esq., now first collected. 3
vols., 1774. Vol. ii.

Fate of Capua. Thomas Southerne. A. 1700. The edition
of Southerne's Works already quoted. Vol. iii.

First Part of the Contention. Marlowe and others(?). P.
1594. Shakespeare's Library, 5 vols., 1875. Vol. v.

Four Elements. Anon. W. 1510–20. Anonymous Plays,
First Series, J. S. Farmer, 1905.

Four Plays in One. Beaumont and Fletcher. A. 1608(?).
P. 1647. The edition used in Beggar's Bush. Vol. x.

Four Ps. John Heywood. P. c. 1545. The Dramatic Writings
of John Heywood, J. S. Farmer, 1905.

Friar Bacon and Friar Bungay. Robert Greene. W. 1589(?).
P. 1594. The edition of Greene's Works already quoted.
Vol. ii.

Friendship in Fashion. Thomas Otway. A. 1678. The
edition of Otway's Works already quoted. Vol. ii.

Gammer Gurton's Needle. W. Stevenson(?). W. 1552–53(?).
P. 1575. Specimens of Pre-Shaksperean Drama, J. M.
Manly. Vol. ii.

Gentleman Usher. George Chapman. A. 1601–2. P. 1606.
The edition of Chapman's Works already quoted. Vol. i.

Giovanni and Annabella. See 'Tis Pity She's a Whore.

God's Promises. Bishop Bale. W. 1538. Dodsley's Old
English Plays. Vol. i.

Golden Age. Thomas Heywood. W. before 1611. P. 1611.
The edition of Heywood's Works already quoted. Vol. iii.

Great Duke of Florence. Philip Massinger. L. 1627. P.
1635. The edition of Massinger's Works already quoted.
Vol. iii.

Greene's Tu Quoque. John Cooke. A. 1611(?). P. 1614.
Hazlitt's Dodsley, vol. xi.

Grim the Collier of Croydon. William Haughton. A. 1600(?).
P. 1662. Anonymous Plays, Fourth Series, J. S. Farmer,
1908.

Guardian. Philip Massinger. L. 1633. P. 1655. The edition of Massinger's Works already quoted. Vol. iv.

Hamlet. William Shakspere. W. 1601(?). S.R. 1602. P. 1603. Folio, 1623.

I Henry IV. William Shakspere. W. *c.* 1597. S.R. 1598. P. 1598. Folio, 1623.

Henry VIII. William Shakspere. W. *c.* 1611. A. 1613 (?). P. 1623. Folio, 1623.

Historical Register. Henry Fielding. A. 1637. One of a Number of Plays Bound Together, 1741.

History of Sir Francis Drake. William Davenant. A. 1659. P. 1659. The edition of Davenant's Works already quoted.

II Honest Whore. Thomas Dekker. W. 1604. S.R. 1608. P. 1630. The Dramatic Works of Thomas Dekker, now first collected with notes and a memoir. 4 vols., 1873. Vol. ii.

How a Man May Choose a Good Wife. Anon. W. 1601. P. 1602. Hazlitt's Dodsley, Vol. ix.

Humorous Lieutenant. John Fletcher. A. 1619. P. 1647. The edition by Glover and Waller already quoted. Vol. ii.

Hycke-Scorner. Anon. P. *c.* 1530. Anonymous Plays, First Series, J. S. Farmer, 1905.

If this be not a good Play, the Devil is in it. Thomas Dekker. W. 1610. P. 1612. The edition of Dekker's Works already quoted. Vol. iii.

I If you Know Not Me. Thomas Heywood. P. 1605. The edition of Heywood's Works already quoted. Vol. i.

Impatient Poverty. Anon. P. 1560. "Lost" Tudor Plays and Some Others, J. S. Farmer, 1907.

Insatiate Countess. John Marston. A. 1610–13. P. 1613. The edition of Marston's Works already quoted. Vol. iii.

Interlude of Youth. Anon. W. 1553–58. Anonymous Plays, Second Series, J. S. Farmer, 1906.

I Iron Age. Thomas Heywood. P. 1632. The edition of Heywood's Works already quoted. Vol. iii.

II Iron Age. Thomas Heywood. P. 1632. The edition
of Heywood's Works already quoted. Vol. iii.

Jack Juggler. Anon. W. between 1553 and 1562. Anonymous Plays. Third Series, J. S. Farmer, 1906.

Jew of Malta. Christopher Marlowe. W. 1588–9. P. 1633.
The edition of Marlowe's Works already quoted.

Johan Johan, Tyb, and Jhon. John Heywood. P. 1533.
The edition of John Heywood's Works already quoted.

John the Evangelist. Anon. W. between 1547 and 1553.
"Lost" Tudor Plays and Some Others, J. S. Farmer,
1907.

King and No King. Beaumont and Fletcher. L. 1611.
P. 1619. The edition of Beaumont and Fletcher's
Works by Glover and Waller. Vol. i.

King Darius. Anon. P. 1565. Anonymous Plays. Third
Series, J. S. Farmer, 1906.

King Lear. William Shakspere. S.R. 1607. P. 1608. Folio, 1623.

King of Lombardy. W. Davenant. W. 1626. Folio, 1673.

Kynge Johan. Bishop Bale. W. c. 1548. Camden Soc. pub.
1838, ed. J. P. Collier.

Like Will to Like. Ulpian Fulwell. P. 1568. Hazlitt's
Dodsley, Vol. iii.

Limberham. John Dryden. A. 1678. The edition of Dryden's Works already quoted.

Looking Glass for London and England. Lodge and Greene.
W. 1589(?). P. 1594. The edition of Greene's Works
already quoted. Vol. i.

Lord Cromwell. Anon. S.R. 1602. P. 1613. Old English
Drama, T. Evan Jacob, 1889.

Love and Honor. William Davenant. L. 1634. P. 1649.
The edition of Davenant's Works already quoted.

Love and Revenge. William Hemings. W. c. 1637. P. 1653.
Quarto, 1675.

Love for Love. William Congreve. P. 1695. The Dramatic
Works of William Congreve, Esq. 1 vol., 1733.

Love in a Nunnery. John Dryden. A. 1672. The edition
of Dryden's Works already quoted.

Love's Sacrifice. John Ford. A. *c.* 1630. P. 1633. The edition of Ford's Works already quoted. Vol. i.

Love Triumphant. John Dryden. A. 1694. The edition of Dryden's Works already quoted.

Loyal Brother. Thomas Southerne. A. 1682. The edition of Southerne's Works already quoted. Vol. i.

Loyal Subject. John Fletcher. L. 1618. P. 1647. The edition of Beaumont and Fletcher's Works by Glover and Waller. Vol. iii.

Lucius Junius Brutus. Nathaniel Lee. A. 1681. The edition of Lee's Works already quoted. Vol. i.

Ludus Coventriae. Anon. MS. of date 1534. Ludus Coventriae. Ed. by J. O. Halliwell, 1841, for the Shakespeare Society.

Lust's Dominion. "Christopher Marlowe." W. 1600(?). P. 1657. The Works of Christopher Marlowe, E. G. Robinson. 3 vols., 1826. Vol. iii.

Lusty Juventus. Richard Wever. W. *c.* 1550. The Dramatic Works of Richard Wever and Thomas Engelend, J. S. Farmer, 1905.

Macbeth. William Shakspeare. W. 1605–6. P. 1623. Folio, 1623.

Macro Plays. Anon. MS. written during the reign of Edward IV. (1461–1483). Macro Plays. Ed. by F. J. Furnivall and A. W. Pollard, in the E. E. T. S., Extra Series. Vol. xci.

Mad Lover. John Fletcher. A. *c.* 1618. P. 1647. The edition of Beaumont and Fletcher's Works by Glover and Waller. Vol. iii.

Magnificence. John Skelton. W., 1515–1523. The Poetical Works of John Skelton; with notes and some account of the author and his writings, Alexander Dyce. 2 vols., 1843. Vol. i.

Maiden Queen. John Dryden. A. 1667. The edition of Dryden's Works already quoted.

Maid's Tragedy. Beaumont and Fletcher. L. 1611. P. 1619. The edition of Beaumont and Fletcher's Works by Glover and Waller. Vol. i.

Mankind. Anon. Fifteenth century. "Lost" Tudor Plays and Some Others, J. S. Farmer, 1907.

Marriage of Wit and Science. Anon. L. 1569–70. Anonymous Plays, Fourth Series, J. S. Farmer, 1908.

Martyred Soldier. Henry Shirley. W. before 1627. P. 1638. Old English Plays, A. H. Bullen. 4 vols., 1882–5. Vol. i.

Mary Magdalene. Anon. MS. of the fifteenth century. The edition of the Digby Mysteries already quoted.

Massacre of Paris. Christopher Marlowe. A. 1593. P. 1594(?). The edition of Marlowe's Works already quoted.

Mayor of Queensborough. Thomas Middleton. W. 1596–7. P. 1661. The edition of Middleton's Works already quoted. Vol. ii.

Menaechmi. Plautus. The edition of Plautus's Comedies already quoted. Vol. i.

Merchant of Venice. William Shakspeare. W. 1594. P. 1600. Folio, 1623.

Merry Beggars, Richard Brome. A. 1641. P. 1652. The edition of Brome's Works already quoted. Vol. iii.

Messallina. Nathaniel Richards. P. 1640. Quarto, 1640.

Michaelmas Term. Thomas Middleton. W. 1604. P. 1607. The edition of Middleton's Works already quoted. Vol. i.

Miles Gloriosus. Plautus. The edition of Plautus's Comedies already quoted. Vol. i.

Mind, Will, and Understanding. Anon. W. in fifteenth century. The edition of the Digby Mysteries already quoted.

Mithridates. Nathaniel Lee. A. 1678. The edition of Lee's Works already quoted. Vol. iii.

Mock Astrologer. See Evening's Love.

Monsieur Thomas. John Fletcher. A. c. 1609. P. 1639. The edition of Beaumont and Fletcher's Works by Glover and Waller. Vol. iv.

More Dissemblers besides Women. Thomas Middleton. A. 1622–3. P. 1657. The edition of Middleton's Works already quoted. Vol. vi.

12

Mundus et Infans. Anon. W. *c.* 1500–1506. P. 1522.
Anonymous Plays, First Series, J. S. Farmer, 1905.

Nature. Henry Medwell. W. in the fifteenth century.
P. 1510–20. "Lost" Tudor Plays and Some Others,
J. S. Farmer, 1907.

New Custom. Anon. W. between 1534 and 1573. Anonymous Plays, Third Series, J. S. Farmer, 1906.

Nice Wanton. "T.R." W. *c.* 1547–1553. P. 1560. Specimens of the Pre-Shaksperean Drama, J. M. Manly.
Vol. i.

Norwich Plays. Only the Grocers' Play extant. Two MSS.
of dates 1534 and 1565. Specimens of the Pre-Shaksperean Drama, J. M. Manly. Vol. i.

Old Fortunatus. Thomas Dekker. W. 1596. P. 1600.
The edition of Dekker's Works already quoted. Vol. i.

Old Law. Middleton and others. A. 1599(?). P. 1656.
The edition of Massinger's Works already quoted. Vol.
iv.

Old Wives' Tale. George Peele. W. 1590(?). P. 1595.
The edition of Peele's Works already quoted. Vol. i.

Outlaw's Christmas. Theodore Kremer. A. 1908.

Parisitaster. John Marston. A. 1604. P. 1606. The edition of Marston's Works already quoted. Vol. ii.

Peregrini. Anon. MS. of the fifteenth century. Specimens
of the Pre-Shaksperean Drama, J. M. Manly. Vol. i.

Phoenix. Thomas Middleton. P. 1607. The edition of
Middleton's Works already quoted. Vol. i.

Picture. Philip Massinger. L. 1629. P. 1630. The edition
of Massinger's Works already quoted. Vol. i.

Pilgrim. John Fletcher. A. 1621–2. P. 1647. The edition
of Beaumont and Fletcher's Works by Glover and Waller.
Vol. v.

Pinner of Wakefield. Robert Greene. W. 1588–92. P. 1599.
The edition of Greene's Works already quoted. Vol. ii.

Platonic Lovers. William Davenant. L. 1635. P. 1636.
The edition of Davenant's Works already quoted.

Play of Love. John Heywood. P. 1533. The edition of
John Heywood's Works already quoted.

Play of the Weather. John Heywood. P. 1533. The edition of John Heywood's Works already quoted.

Queen Hester. Anon. P. 1561. Anonymous Plays, Second Series, J. S. Farmer, 1906.

Ralph Roister Doister. Nicholas Udall. W. 1552–3(?). Specimens of the Pre-Shakspearean Drama, J. M. Manly. Vol. ii.

Rape of Lucrece. Thomas Heywood. A. c. 1605. P. 1608. The edition of Heywood's Works already quoted. Vol. v.

Rehearsal. George Villiers, Duke of Buckingham. A. 1671. The Rehearsal, E. Arber (English Reprints, 1869).

Renegado. Philip Massinger. L. 1624. P. 1630(?). The edition of Massinger's Works already quoted. Vol. ii.

Respublica. Anon. W. 1553. "Lost" Tudor Plays and Some Others, J. S. Farmer, 1907.

Resurrection Play. Anon. W. in the twelfth century. The Prologue is given in Chambers' Mediæval Stage, pp. 82–3.

Roman Actor. Philip Massinger. A. 1626. P. 1629. The edition of Massinger's Works already quoted. Vol. i.

Romeo and Juliet. William Shakspere. W. 1591–6 P. 1597. Folio, 1623.

Roxana. William Alabaster. P. 1632. Quarto, 1632.

Royal King and Loyal Subject. Thomas Heywood. W. 1618(?). P. 1637. The edition of Heywood's Works already quoted. Vol. vi.

Sapho and Phao. John Lyly. W. 1581. P. 1584. The Complete Works of John Lyly, now first collected and edited from the earliest quartos, with life, bibliography, essays, notes, and index, R. W. Bond. 3 vols., 1902. Vol. ii.

Satiro-Mastix. Thomas Dekker. A. 1601. P. 1602. The edition of Dekker's Works already quoted. Vol. i.

Scholar. R. Lovelace. W. 1636(?). P. (Prologue and Epilogue) 1649. Poems of Richard Lovelace, W. Carew Hazlitt, 1864.

Sejanus. Ben Jonson. A. 1603. S.R. 1604. P. 1605.

The edition of Jonson's Works already quoted. Vol. i.

She Would if She Could. Sir George Etheredge. A. 1668. The Works of Sir George Etheredge, containing his Plays and Poems, 1 vol., 1735.

Siege of Rhodes. William Davenant. A. 1656. P. 1656. The edition of Davenant's Works already quoted.

Silver Age. Thomas Heywood. P. 1613. The edition of Heywood's Works already quoted. Vol. iii.

Sir Martin Mar-All. John Dryden. A. 1667. The edition of Dryden's Works already quoted.

Soldier's Fortune. Thomas Otway. P. 1681. The edition of Otway's Works already quoted. Vol. ii.

Sophonisba. John Marston. A. 1602–3. P. 1606. The edition of Marston's Works already quoted. Vol. ii.

Spanish Friar. John Dryden. A. 1681. The edition of Dryden's Works already quoted.

Spanish Tragedy. Thomas Kyd. W. 1586(?). P. 1594. The works of Thomas Kyd, F. S. Boas. 1 vol., 1901.

Summoning of Everyman. Anon. P. before 1531. Anonymous Plays, First Series, J. S. Farmer, 1905.

Tale of a Tub. Ben Jonson. W. 1601(?). P. 1640. The edition of Jonson's Works already quoted. Vol. ii.

I Tamburlaine. Christopher Marlowe. W. 1587. P. 1592. The edition of Marlowe's Works already quoted.

II Tamburlaine. Christopher Marlowe. W. 1587. P. 1592 The edition of Marlowe's Works already quoted.

Thersites. Anon. A. 1537. P. 1561(?). Anonymous Plays, First Series, J. S. Farmer, 1905.

'Tis Pity She's a Whore. John Ford. A. c. 1626. P. 1633. The edition of Ford's Works already quoted. Vol. i.

Titus and Berenice. Thomas Otway. A. 1677. The edition of Otway's Works already quoted. Vol. i.

Towneley, Plays. Anon. MS. of the fifteenth century. The Towneley Plays, G. England and A. W. Pollard, 1897. E. E. T. S. Vol. lxxi., Extra Series.

Trial of Treasure. Anon. P. 1567. Anonymous Plays, Second Series, J. S. Farmer, 1906.

Trick to Catch the Old One. Thomas Middleton. A. 1606.

P. 1608. The edition of Middleton's Works already quoted. Vol. ii.

Tyrannic Love. John Dryden. P. 1670. The edition of Dryden's Works already quoted.

Unnatural Combat. Philip Massinger. W. 1621. P. 1639. The edition of Massinger's Works already quoted. Vol. iii.

Valentinian. John Fletcher. W. 1617. P. 1647. The edition of Beaumont and Fletcher's Works by Glover and Waller. Vol. iv.

Variety. William Cavendish, Duke of Newcastle. A. 1639–40. P. 1649.

Venice Preserved. Thomas Otway. A. 1682. The edition of Otway's Works already quoted. Vol. iii.

Virgin Prophetess. Elkanah Settle. A. 1701. Quarto, 1701.

Virgin Martyr. Philip Massinger. L. 1620. P. 1621. The edition of Massinger's Works already quoted. Vol. i.

Volpone. Ben Jonson. A. 1606. P. 1607. The edition of Jonson's Works already quoted. Vol. i.

Wealth and Health. Anon. P. 1565(?). "Lost" Tudor Plays and Some Others, J. S. Farmer, 1907.

What You Will. John Marston. W. 1601(?). P. 1607. The edition of Marston's Works already quoted. Vol. ii.

White Devil. John Webster. A. 1607(?). P. 1612. The White Devil and The Duchess of Malfy by John Webster, M. W. Sampson, 1904.

Whore of Babylon. Thomas Dekker. W. 1605(?). P. 1607. The edition of Dekker's Works already quoted. Vol. ii.

Widow's Tears. George Chapman. A. 1605. P. 1612. The edition of Chapman's Works already quoted. Vol. iii.

Wife for a Month. John Fletcher. L. 1624. P. 1647. The edition of Beaumont and Fletcher's Works by Glover and Waller. Vol. v.

Wild Gallant. John Dryden. A. 1663. The edition of Dryden's Works already quoted.

Wise Woman of Hogsdon. Thomas Heywood. A. 1604. P. 1638. The edition of Heywood's Works already quoted. Vol. v.

Wisdom of Doctor Dodypoll.   George Peele(?).   A. *c.* 1590(?).
P. 1600.   Old English Plays, A. H. Bullen.   Vol. iii.

Wit and Science.   John Redford.   W. *c.* 1545.   "Lost" Tudor Plays and Some Others, J. S. Farmer, 1907.

Wit without Money.   John Fletcher.   A. 1614.   P. 1639.
The edition of Beaumont and Fletcher's Works by Glover and Waller.   Vol. ii.

Witch.   Thomas Middleton.   A. *c.* 1621(?).   The edition of Middleton's Works already quoted.   Vol. v.

Witch of Edmonton.   Rowley, Dekker, and Ford.   A. *c.* 1621.   P. 1658.   The edition of Dekker's Works already quoted.   Vol. iv.

Witches of Lancashire.   Thomas Heywood.   A. 1634.   P. 1634.   The edition of Heywood's Works already quoted. Vol. iv.

Wits, or Sport upon Sport.   Collected by Francis Kirkman.
P. 1672-3.   Quarto, 1673.

Women beware Women.   Thomas Middleton.   W. *c.* 1612(?).
P. 1657.   The edition of Middleton's Works already quoted.   Vol. vi.

York Plays.   MS. 1430-1440.   York Plays.   Ed. by L. Toulmin Smith, 1885.

INDEX

INDEX